THE

ERRORS OF ROMANISM,

&c.

THE
ERRORS OF ROMANISM

TRACED TO

THEIR ORIGIN

IN

HUMAN NATURE.

BY

RICHARD WHATELY, D.D.

PRINCIPAL OF ST. ALBAN'S HALL, AND LATE FELLOW OF ORIEL
COLLEGE, OXFORD.

The thing that hath been, it is that which shall be; and that which is done, is that which shall be done: and there is no new thing under the sun. *Eccles.* i. 9.

.... γιγνόμενα μὲν, καὶ ἀεὶ ἐσόμενα, ἕως ἂν Ἡ ΑΥΤΗ ΦΥΣΙΣ ΑΝΘΡΩΠΩΝ ᾖ, μᾶλλον δὲ καὶ ἡσυχαίτερα, καὶ τοῖς εἴδεσι διηλλαγμένα, ὡς ἂν ἕκασται αἱ μεταβολαὶ τῶν ξυντυχιῶν ἐφιστῶνται. Thucyd. b. iii. ch. 82.

LONDON:
B. FELLOWES, LUDGATE STREET.
1830.

BAXTER, PRINTER, OXFORD.

TO

THE REVEREND

JOSEPH BLANCO WHITE, M.A.

OF ORIEL COLLEGE, OXFORD.

My dear Friend,

I AM aware that it is a violation of established forms to take the liberty of dedicating this Work to you, without previously applying for your permission.

The ground on which I petition for your indulgence, is, my fear that your modesty might have led you, if not to withhold your consent altogether, yet to prohibit me from speaking of you in the manner I could wish. Not that it is my design to make this Dedication the vehicle of a formal panegyric; or to comment either on that part of your character and conduct which is before the public, and which it would be an affront to my readers to suppose them not to know and admire; or again, on the particulars of our private friendship, in which they have no concern. But I feel bound to take this occasion of acknowledging publicly one particular advantage which I have derived from my intercourse with you: I am indebted to you for such an insight into the peculiarities of the Church of Rome, as I could never have gained, either from any one who had not been originally, or from any one who still continued, a member of that Church. Your intimate acquaintance with it, has enlarged and cleared the view I had long since taken of its system; as being the gradual, spontaneous growth of the human heart;—as being, what may be called, in a certain sense, the *Religion of Nature;* viz. such a kind of religion as "the natural Man" is disposed to frame for himself.

One who has both been so deeply versed as yourself in the learning of that Church, and has also had the opportunities you have enjoyed, of not merely forming a judgment of the apparent *tendencies* of each part of the system, but observing how it *actually* works, and what are the practical results—and who has subsequently been enabled, under the divine blessing, to embrace a purer faith—must, unless he fall far short of you in candour or intelligence, be much better qualified than either a Romanist, or one brought up in our Church, to estimate the true character of the two Religions. As, on the one hand, (like Moses, who was "skilled in all the learning of the Egyptians,") you may be reckoned, as far as knowledge is concerned, an eminent Roman-Catholic Divine, so, on the other hand, you may, in one point of view, be considered as more eminently Protestant, than most members of our Church. For I cannot, of course, be certain, of others, or even of myself, that, if we had, like you, been educated in the Romish Church, we should have escaped, like you, from that spiritual bondage;—that we might not have either continued enslaved to her tenets, or have been plunged irrecoverably into that gulf of Atheism, to the brink of which She brings her votaries: which She does, as you have well pointed out, by sedulously presenting as the sole alternative, implicit devotion to her decrees, or, no religion at all.

It is, as I have said, impossible to pronounce with certainty, of any one bred a Protestant, that he would have *become* so, had he been educated in the Romish system: but it might safely be pronounced, that I should *not* have done so, were I one of those who stigmatize you as an Apostate, for renouncing and testifying against the system in which you were brought up. I should then deserve to be characterised as Protestant only by the accidents of Country and Kindred.

You are doubtless familiar however with the principle long since noticed by the great Historian of Greece, and ready to make allowance for its operation, that " most men are slow to give another credit for feeling nobler sentiments, and acting on higher motives, than any that have ever found a place in their own breasts ª." Posterity nevertheless will, I am convinced, do justice to your character, and appreciate your services.

Diram qui contudit *Hydram*,
Comperit invidiam supremo fine domari.

ª ―― εἴτι ὑπὲρ τὴν ἑαυτοῦ φύσιν ἀκούοι. μέχρι γὰρ τοῦδε ἀνεκτοὶ οἱ ἔπαινοί εἰσι περὶ ἑτέρων λεγόμενοι, ἐς ὅσον ἂν καὶ αὐτὸς ἕκαστος οἴηται ἱκανὸς εἶναι δρᾶσαι τι ὧν ἤκουσε· τῷ δὲ ὑπερβάλλοντι αὐτῶν φθονοῦντες, ἤδη καὶ ἀπιστοῦσιν. Thucyd. b. ii. ch. 35.

You have been led, by the circumstances in which you were placed, and of which you have taken due advantage, to examine different systems carefully, and to make up your mind on mature deliberation. And the same circumstances which induced you to observe, and enabled you to estimate, the *differences* between Romanists and Protestants, have also qualified you to notice the points of *resemblance* in all men; to recognize in all, of whatever country or persuasion, the tendency towards each of those Romish errors which you have seen magnified and exaggerated in that Church;—to detect the minutest drop, in the most disguised mixture, of those poisons which you have seen in their rectified and concentrated form, operating to produce their baneful results.

With a view therefore to the particular object of the present work, it must have been very much my own fault, if I have not derived from your conversation, the most valuable suggestions and corrections. I only regret that you did not yourself undertake the task, for which no one else can be, on the whole, so well qualified.

As it is, I have only to express thus publicly my sense of the advantages I have enjoyed, and to beg your favourable acceptance of this dedication of a Work, to which you will thus have, indirectly, so much contributed. Should I be enabled, by placing in a somewhat new light, questions which have been long since copiously discussed, to awaken the attention even of a few, whether Romanists or Protestants, to the faults, either existing, or likely to arise, among them, you will, I am sure, rejoice to have had a share in contributing to such an effect, and to have your name connected with a Work which shall have produced it. At all events, you will, I am sure, give me credit for good intentions:

nor will you, I trust, be either surprised or mortified, if I should have to encounter, on this occasion especially, (the views set forth being far from flattering to human nature,) some of that opposition of various kinds, and from various quarters, with which many of my former publications have been assailed, and from which yours have not been exempt.

To myself this is not a matter of wonder, or of dissatisfaction. Not that I have any wish to excite controversy; or any intention of ever engaging in it: but he who endeavours to inculcate any neglected truths, or to correct any prevailing errors, must be prepared, if he succeed in attracting any share of public attention, to encounter more or less of opposition. It would be most extravagant to expect to convince at once, if at all, every one, or even many, who before thought differently. If therefore, in such a case, he meet with no opposition, he may take that as a sign either that he has excited no interest at all, or that he was mistaken as to the state of the prevailing opinions among others, or that his own have not been fully understood. Opposition does not indeed, of itself, prove either that he is right, or that he is wrong: but, at all events, the discussion which results, is likely, if conducted with temper and sincerity, to lead to the ascertainment of the truth.

And it is worth remarking, that in many cases the opposition will appear even greater than it really is. For as the great majority of those who had before thought differently from an Author, will, in general, continue to think so, and of course will be prepared, at once, loudly to censure him; so those, whether many or few, who are induced to alter, or to doubt, their former opinion, will seldom be found very forward to proclaim the change, at least till after a considerable interval. Even the most candid and modest, if they are also cautious, will seldom decidedly make up their minds anew, except slowly and gradually.

Hence it often happens, I believe, that while men are led, naturally enough, to estimate the effect produced by any Work, from the comparative numbers and weight of those who applaud, and those who censure it, it shall, in fact, have produced little or no effect on either: those whom it may have really influenced, in bringing them to reconsider their former opinions, being rather disposed, for the most part, to say little about it.

Such as have maintained notions at variance with mine, in Christian meekness and candour, may be assured of my perfect good-will towards them, and of my earnest wish that whichever of us is in the right, may succeed in establishing his conclusions. As for any who may have assailed, or who may hereafter assail me, with unchristian bitterness, or with sophistical misrepresentation, much as I of course lament that such weapons should ever be employed at all, I can truly say, (and I doubt not you will say the same for yourself,) that I had far rather see them employed against me, than on my side. There is also this consolatory reflection for any one who is so attacked: that weak or sophistical arguments are then the most likely to be resorted to, when better cannot be found;—that one who indulges in invective, affords some kind of presumption, that he at least can find no such reasons as are even to himself satisfactory;—and that misrepresentation is the natural resource of those who find the positions they are determined to oppose, to be such, that if fairly stated, and fully understood, they could not be overthrown. Such attacks, therefore, tend rather, as far as they go, to support, than to weaken, in the judgment of rational inquirers, the cause against which they are directed.

You may have observed too, that there are some particular charges often brought, without proof, against an Author, which are not only unfounded, but are occasioned by qualities the very reverse of those imputed. You may have heard a Writer censured as "sophistical," precisely because he is *not* sophistical; and as "dogmatical," *because* he is not dogmatical. With a Work that is really sophistical, the obvious procedure is, either to pass it by with contempt, or, if the fallacies seem worth noticing, to detect and expose them. But if men find the arguments opposed to them to be such, that they cannot *prove* them sophistical, it is yet easy (and it is not unnatural) at least to *call* them so. The phrase "sophistical arguments," accordingly, is often in reality equivalent to, "such as I would fain answer, but cannot." Not that in such cases the imputation is necessarily insincere, or even necessarily false. One whose reasoning-powers are not strong, may really suspect, though he cannot point it out, a latent fallacy in some argument which leads to a conclusion he objects to; and it may so happen that his suspicion is right, and that a fallacy may exist which he has not the skill to detect. But then, he is not justified in *pronouncing* the argument sophistical, till he is prepared to make good the charge. A verdict without evidence, must always be unjust, whether the accused be, in fact, innocent or guilty.

Dogmatism again, to speak strictly, consists in assertions without proof. But one who does really thus dogmatize, you may have often seen received with more toleration than might have been anticipated. Those who think with him, often derive some degree of satisfaction from the confirmation thus afforded to their opinion, though not by any fresh argument, yet by an implied assent to such as have convinced themselves: those again who think differently, feel that the Author has merely declared his sentiments, and (provided his language be not insolent and overbearing) has left them in undisturbed possession of their own. Not so, one who supports his opinions by cogent reasons: he seems by so doing to call on them either to refute the arguments, or to alter their own views. And however mildly he may express himself, they are sometimes displeased at the molestation thus inflicted, by one who is not content merely to think as he pleases, leaving others to do the same, but seems aiming to compel others (the very word " cogent," as applied to reasons, seems to denote this character) to think with him, whether they like it or not. And this displeasure one may often hear vented in the application of the title " dogmatical;" which denotes, when so applied, the exact reverse of dogmatism; viz. that the Author is not satisfied with simply declaring his own opinions; (which is really dogmatism;) but, by the reasoning he employs, calls on others to adopt them.

I am aware, however, that truth may be advocated, and by sound arguments, in a needlessly offensive form. It has always been my aim to avoid, as far as may be without a sinful compromise of truth, every thing tending to excite hostile feelings, either within or without the pale of my own Church. And I cherish a hope, that I may have done something in the present Work towards softening the feelings of the candid among Romanists and Protestants, towards each other. I have not indeed attempted this, by labouring to extenuate or explain away the erroneousness of the Romish tenets and practices; because this would imply, according to my views, a sacrifice of truth. But to trace those errors to the principles of our common Nature, and, while we strongly censure the faults themselves, to acknowledge our own ever-besetting danger of falling into the like, is, I trust, a more conciliating, as I am convinced it is a truer, view of the subject, than to cast the whole burden of blame on a particular Church, and to exult in our own supposed perfection.

You will recognize in the following pages a series of Discourses delivered before the University, and the whole or the greater part of which, you heard. I have inserted passages in several parts; but have made, on the whole, little other alterations. It would not have been difficult to give the Work more of a systematic form, and to adopt a style more removed from that which is suited to delivery: but I was inclined to think, that such alterations would have had no tendency to make the subject better understood, and might rather have lessened the interest of it. I accordingly determined to print the whole very nearly as it was delivered.

The views I have taken are not anticipated in any work I am acquainted with. Several writers indeed have glanced slightly, incidentally, and partially, at the principle here attempted to be established, or have advanced some steps towards it. Bp. Lavington has compared a part of the Romish errors with those of some modern enthusiasts; and Middleton, another part, with those of the ancient Pagans; but they have stopped short of the general conclusion to which my own observations and reflections, combined with yours, have led me.

I have, however, availed myself, in several instances, of the suggestions of various Writers; to whom, as far as my memory would serve, I have made reference. It so happens, that some of these, including yourself, are living Authors whom I have the pleasure of knowing personally: and I am not sure that I may not, on that ground, incur censure for citing them with approbation; as if I must unavoidably be biassed by partial feelings. I would rather, however, incur the suspicion of such partiality, than of not daring to do that justice to a friend which would be due to a stranger. And it should in fairness be remembered, that though it is very possible to overrate a friend, yet, as it is also possible that a writer of real merit may possess personal friends, so, it would be hard that this should necessarily operate to his disadvantage, by precluding them from bearing just testimony in his favour.

Once more I intreat you to accept my apology for the liberty I have taken, and to believe me,

With deep-felt esteem and veneration,
    Your faithful and affectionate Friend,

RICHARD WHATELY.

CONTENTS.

CHAP. I.
OF SUPERSTITION.

§. 1. Apparent strangeness of the transgressions of the Israelites, 1. difficulty of rightly estimating the temptations of those far removed from us, 5.

§. 2. Lessons to be learned from the example of the Church of Rome, 9. errors of that Church gradual and imperceptible in their rise, 11.

§ 3. Principal Romish errors; Superstition, 12. fondness for speculative mysteries, 13. and for vicarious service of God, 14. sanction given to deceit, 15. claim to infallibility, 16. persecution, 17. confidence in the title of Catholic, 18.

§. 4. Danger of falling into corresponding faults, 19.

§. 5. Resemblance between the superstitions of the Israelites and of the Romanists, 22. definition of Superstition, 26. false security against it, 30.

§. 6. Mischiefs of Superstition, 33.

§. 7. Connection of Superstition with profaneness, 40.

§. 8. Occasions of Superstition, 45.

§. 9. Superstitious belief in miracles, 49. superstitions connected with the Eucharist, 51. with Baptism, 55. with Prayer, 58. with rites of interment, 68.

§. 10. Cautions to be used against the inroads of Superstition, 71.

CHAP. II.
OF VICARIOUS RELIGION.

§. 1. Character of Christian Mysteries, 77. natural tendency to set up two kinds of religion; for the priests, and for the people, 80. speculative theology of philosophizing divines, 83.

§. 2. Real origin and progress of priestcraft, 89.

§. 3. Distinct characters of Hiereus and Presbyteros, 94.

§. 4. Offices of the Jewish and the Pagan priests, 97.

§, 5. Character and offices of Christian Ministers, 102.

§. 6. Mistakes and misrepresentations arising from confounding the two offices, 108.

§. 7. Change of the Christian priesthood by the Church of Rome, 111.

§. 8. Tendency to discountenance the education of the poor, 114. mistakes as to what is meant by embracing Christianity, 117. and as to the relation of Pastors and Flocks, 122.

§. 9. Proneness of the People to vicarious religion, 123.

§. 10. Professional distinctions between Clergy and Laity, how far desirable, 126.

§. 11. Mistakes as to what is a good *example*, 131.

CHAP. III.
OF PIOUS FRAUDS.

§. 1. Deceit employed by the Jews against the Christians, 135.

§. 2. Tendency to justify frauds employed for a good end, 141.

§. 3. Connection of this fault with the one treated of in the foregoing chapter, 145. self-deceit the final result, 147.

§. 4. Difficulty of appreciating the strength of the temptations to falsehood in times or countries remote from our own, 148. importance of a vivid Imagination, in the study of History, 151.

§. 5. Division of frauds into negative and positive: and again, into falsehood in what is maintained, and in the reasons by which it is maintained, 152.

§. 6. Illustrations from conceivable cases of temptation to deceit; in keeping up the pretension to inspiration, 156. in conniving at false grounds for right belief, 159. or for right practice, 160. in administering groundless consolations, &c. 163.

§. 7. Ultimate inexpediency of fraud, 166.

CHAP. IV.

OF UNDUE RELIANCE ON HUMAN AUTHORITY.

§. 1. Claim of the Romish Church to infallibility, not originally the *consequence* of misinterpretation of Scripture-texts, 169.

§. 2. Reasonings and texts of Scripture often called in to justify practices or opinions previously subsisting, 173.

§. 3. Natural tendency to appeal to an infallible guide, 180.

§. 4. Presumption in favour of the tenets of the wise and good, or of the Catholic Church, 184.

§. 5. Alleged claim of infallibility by Protestant Churches, 189. refuted, 191. ambiguity of the word " authority," 193.

§. 6. Evil consequences of the claim to infallibility, 194. danger of Protestants on this point, 197. office of Churches to supply what the sacred writers purposely omitted, 199. reasons for the omission, 201.

§. 7. Arguments in favour of an habitual appeal to human formularies, 203. answered, 204. dangers of the practice, 209.

§. 8. Temptations to set up a virtual claim to infallibility, 213.

CHAP. V.
OF PERSECUTION.

§. 1. Men responsible to God, and to Him alone, for the rejection of divine truth, 221. and only in the next life, 223.

§. 2. Importance of right principles for avoiding the two errors, of intolerance, and indifference, 227.

§. 3. Mistakes as to what constitutes the spirit of persecution; which does not consist either in the tenet that the salvation of heretics is impossible, 231. or in maintaining the wrong side, 236. or in excessive severity, 237. or in revengeful motives, 238. or in punishing *opinions*, 239. or in actual *infliction* of punishment, 241.

§. 4. How heretics are to be treated, conformably with the character of Christ's kingdom, 245. attempts to explain away his declarations and precepts, 247.

§. 5. Scriptural arguments against intolerance, to be preferred, for popular use, 251.

§. 6. Blindness of many reasoners to the abstract arguments against it, 256.

§. 7. Causes of the greater hostility often felt against infidels and heretics, than against the vicious, 258. comparative unfrequency of avowed infidelity, 260. support derived from authority, shaken, 261. personal affront to the Christian's understanding, implied by the infidel, 263. suspicion of moral corruption as biassing the infidel's judgment, 264.

§. 8. Extent and influence of this hostile feeling, 265.

§. 9. Reasons for believing that anti-christians would be tempted into persecution, 272. true Christianity the only effectual security against it, 277.

§. 10. What things are liable to be falsely regarded as necessarily implying intolerance; refusing to admit, in every case, the plea of conscience, 278. union of civil with spiritual or ecclesiastical office, 283. requisition of a certain religious persuasion as a condition of personal friendship, or of any thing to which there existed previously no claim of *right*, 286. defence against aggression, 293. which must not however be expected to exempt the sincere Christian from mortifying opposition, 295.

CHAP. VI.
OF TRUST IN NAMES AND PRIVILEGES.

§. 1. Disposition of the ancient Jews to rely on their privileges and titles, 299.

§. 2. Tendency to the same fault in the primitive Christians, 302.

§. 3. Exemplification of the universality of this tendency, from the Romish Church, 305.

§. 4. Danger of a corresponding nature exists equally among Protestants, 312.

§. 5. Recapitulation of the several points in which we may take warning from the example of the Romanists, 315.

§. 6. Cautions to be used in guarding against undue reliance on the sanctity of the Titles we bear, and the Societies we belong to, 321.

APPENDIX.

[A.] On the application of the term CATHOLIC to designate "a member of the Church of Rome," 327.

[B.] On "Self-righteousness," and other kinds of Spiritual-pride, 335. "Auricular Confession," 345. Impossibility of framing such a self-preserving system, as shall supersede personal vigilance, 346.

THE ERRORS OF ROMANISM

TRACED TO

THEIR ORIGIN

IN

HUMAN NATURE.

CHAP. I.
SUPERSTITION.

§. 1. THERE are few things probably that appear at the first glance more strange to a reader of the Old Testament, than the frequent lapses of the Israelites into idolatrous and other superstitious practices;—the encouragement or connivance often granted to these by such of the rulers as were by no means altogether destitute of piety;— and the warm commendations which are accordingly bestowed on such of their kings as avoided and repressed these offences. Their Law had been delivered and its authority maintained with such strikingly awful solemnity, and its directions were so precise and minute, that a strict conformity to it appears, to us, hardly to amount to a virtue, and the violation of it, to an almost incredible infatuation. It is not without a considerable mental effort that we can so far transport ourselves into the situation of persons living in so very different a condition of society from our own, as to estimate duly the nature and the force of the temptations to which they were exposed, to make fair allowance for their backslidings, and to bestow adequate applause on those of them who adhered stedfastly to the Divine commands.

The conduct of Hezekiah, for instance, who " removed the high-places, and brake the images, and cut down the groves, and brake in pieces the brazen serpent that Moses had made; (for unto those days the children of Israel did burn incense to it;)" is likely perhaps to strike some readers as so far from being any heroic effort of virtue, that the chief wonder is, how his predecessors and their subjects could have been so strangely remiss and disobedient, as to leave him so much to do. Things however being in such a state, the duty of remedying at once the abuses which had grown up, is apt to strike us, at first sight, as so very obvious and imperative, that we are hardly disposed to give him due praise for fulfilling it. But the more attentively we consider the times in which he lived, and the peculiar circumstances in which he began his reign—the successor of an idolatrous prince, and reigning over an idolatrous people—the higher admiration we shall feel for his exemplary obedience to the divine law.

It should be remembered, that not only the avowed violators of the first Commandment, but those also, who, though they transgressed the second, yet professed themselves the worshippers of Jehovah exclusively, would be likely to tax with *impiety* that unsparing reform of abuses, which even those former kings, who are described as "doing that which was right in the sight of the Lord," had yet not ventured to undertake. Indeed his enemy Sennacherib reproaches him on this very ground: "if ye say, We trust in the Lord our God, is not that he whose high-places and whose altars Hezekiah hath taken away?"

But many, even of those who perhaps endured his putting a stop to the irregular and unauthorized worship of Jehovah in those high-places, might yet be scandalized at his venturing to destroy the brazen serpent; an emblem framed originally by Divine command, and which had been the appointed and supernatural means of a miraculous deliverance. If such a relic were even *now* in existence, and its identity indisputable, it would not be contemplated, by any believer in the Mosaic history, without some degree of veneration. How much stronger would that veneration be in the mind of an Israelite, and of one in that ignorant and semi-barbarous age! Yet one of these was found sufficiently enlightened to estimate the evil, and bold enough to use the effectual remedy. The king is not content to forbid this idolatrous use of the image, or even to seclude it carefully from the public gaze; it had been an occasion of superstition, and he " brake it in pieces;" applying to it at the same time the contemptuous appellation of " piece of brass[a]," in order to destroy more completely that reverence which had degenerated into a sin.

Men are apt, not only in what regards religion, but in respect of *all* human concerns, to con-

---

[a] " He called it Nehushtan." 2 Kings xviii. 4.

template the faults and follies of a distant age or country, with barren wonder, or with self-congratulating contempt; while they overlook, because they do not search for, perhaps equal, and even corresponding, vices and absurdities in their own conduct. And in this way it is that the religious, and moral, and political, lessons which history may be made to furnish, are utterly lost to the generality of mankind. Human nature is always and every where, in the most important points, substantially the same; circumstantially and externally, men's manners and conduct are infinitely various, in various times and regions. If the former were not true—if it were not for this fundamental agreement—history could furnish no instruction; if the latter were not true—if there were not these apparent and circumstantial differences—hardly any one could fail to profit by that instruction. For few are so dull as not to learn something from the records of past experience in cases precisely similar to their own. But as it is, much candour and diligence are called for in tracing the analogy between cases which, at the first glance, seem very different—in observing the workings of the same human nature under all its various disguises—in recognizing, as it were, the same plant in different stages of its growth, and in all the varieties resulting from climate and culture, soil and season.

But to any one who *will* employ this diligence and candour, this very dissimilarity of circumstances renders the history of past times and distant countries, even the more instructive; because it is easier to form an impartial judgment concerning them. The difficulty is to apply that judgment to the cases before us. In contemplating human transactions, the law of optics is reversed; we see the most indistinctly the objects which are close around us; we view them through the discoloured medium of our own prejudices and passions; the more familiar we are with them, the less truly do we estimate their real colours and dimensions. Transactions and characters the most unconnected with ourselves—the most remote from all that presents itself in our own times, and at home, appear before us with all their deformities unveiled, and display their intrinsic and essential qualities. We are even liable to attend so exclusively to this intrinsic and abstract character of remote events, as to make too *little* allowance (while in recent cases we make too much) for the circumstances in which the agents were placed; and thence to regard as instances of almost incredible folly or depravity, things not fundamentally very different from what is passing around us.

And as the law of optics is in this case reversed, our procedure must be reversed accordingly. We judge of the nature of distant objects, by an examination of those near at hand, whose similarity to the others we have ascertained. So also must we on the contrary learn to judge impartially of our own conduct and character, and of the events of our own times, by finding parallels to these in cases the most remote and apparently dissimilar; of which, for that reason, our views are the most distinct, and our judgments the most unbiassed; and then, conjecturing what a wise and good man, ten centuries hence, would be likely to pronounce of *us*.

The errors and the vices, among the rest, the superstitions, of the Israelites and again of our ancestors under the Romish Church, did not, we may be sure, appear to them in the same light that they now do to us. No one believes his own opinions to be erroneous, or his own practices superstitious; few are even accustomed to ask themselves, "Is there not a lie in my right hand?" Since therefore our predecessors did not view their doctrines and practices in the same light that we do, this should lead us, not to regard them with contemptuous astonishment and boastful exultation, but rather, to reflect that, like them, we also are likely to form a wrong estimate of what is around us and familiar to our minds: it should teach us to make use of the examples of others, not for the nourishment of pride, but for the detection of our own faults.

We are taught that Satan "transformeth himself into an angel of light;" but he does not use always and every where the same disguise; as soon as one is seen through, he is ready to assume another; and it is in vain that we detect the artifice which has done its work on other men, unless we are on our guard against the same Tempter under some new transformation;—assuming afresh among ourselves the appearance of some angel of light.

§. 2. These reflections are perhaps the more particularly profitable at the present time, on account of the especial attention which has of late been directed to the superstitions, and other errors and enormities, of the Romish Church. Unless such principles as I have adverted to are continually present to the mind, the more our thoughts are, by frequent discussion, turned to the errors of that Church, and to the probability, under this or that conjuncture of circumstances, of proselytes joining that Church, or being gained over from it, the less shall we be on our guard against the *spirit* of popery in the human heart—against similar faults in some different shapes; and the more shall we be apt to deem every danger of the kind effectually escaped, by simply keeping out of the pale of that corrupt Church.

It is indeed in *all* cases profitable to contemplate the errors of other men, if we do this " not high-minded but fearful;"—not for the sake of uncharitable triumph, but with a view to self-examination; even as the Corinthians were exhorted by their Apostle to draw instruction from the backslidings of the Israelites, which were recorded, he says, " for their admonition," to the intent that they might not fall into corresponding sins, and that " he who thought he stood might take heed lest he fell." In all cases, I say, *some* benefit may be derived from *such* a contemplation of the faults of others; but the errors of the Romanists, if examined with a view to our own improvement, will the more effectually furnish this instruction, inasmuch as those errors more especially, will be found to be the natural and spontaneous growth of the human heart; they are (as I have elsewhere remarked) not so much the effect, as the cause, of the Romish system of religion. The peculiar character of Romanism, in this respect will be best perceived by contrasting it with Mahometism; this latter system was framed, and introduced, and established, within a very short space of time, by a deliberately-designing impostor; who did indeed most artfully accommodate that system to man's nature, but did not wait for the gradual and spontaneous operations of human nature to produce it. He reared at once the standard of proselytism, and imposed on his followers a code of doctrines and laws ready-framed for their reception. The tree which he planted did indeed find a congenial soil; but he planted it at once, with its trunk full-formed and its branches displayed: the Romish system, on the contrary, rose insensibly like a young plant from the seed, making a progress scarcely perceptible from year to year, till at length it had fixed its root deeply in the soil, and spread its baneful shade far around.

> Infecunda quidem, sed læta et fortia surgunt;
> Quippe solo natura subest;

it was the natural offspring of man's frail and corrupt character, and it needed no sedulous culture. No one accordingly can point out any precise period at which this " mystery of iniquity"—the system of Romish corruptions—first began, or specify any person who introduced it: no one in fact ever did introduce any such system: the corruptions crept in one by one; originating for the most part with an ignorant and depraved *people*, but connived at, cherished, consecrated, and successively established, by a debased and worldly-minded ministry; and modified by them just so far as might best favour the views of their profligate ambition. But the system thus gradually compacted, was not the deliberate contrivance of any one man or set of men, adepts in priestcraft, and foreseeing and designing the entire result. The corruptions of the Romish Church were the natural offspring of human passions, not checked and regulated by those who ought to have been ministers of the Gospel, but who, on the contrary, were ever ready to indulge and encourage men's weakness and wickedness, provided they could turn it to their own advantage. The good seed " fell among thorns ;" which, being fostered by those who should have been occupied in rooting them out, not only " sprang up with it," but finally choked and overpowered it.

§. 3. The character accordingly of the Romish corruptions is precisely such as the history of that Church would lead us to anticipate.

I. One of the greatest blemishes, for instance, in the Church of Rome, is that which I have already alluded to, superstitious worship; a fault which every one must acknowledge to be the spontaneous and every-where-abundant produce of the corrupt soil of man's heart. The greater part indeed of the errors of Romanism, which I shall hereafter notice under separate heads, may be considered as so many branches of Superstition, or at least inseparably connected with it; but there are besides, many superstitions more strictly so called, with which that system is justly chargeable; such as invocation of saints, and adoration of images and relics; corresponding to that idolatrous practice which King Hezekiah so piously and boldly suppressed.

II. The desire again of prying into mysteries relative to the invisible world, but which have no connection with practice, is another characteristic of human nature, (on which I have elsewhere offered some remarks [b],) and one to which may be traced, the immense mass of presumptuous speculations about things unrevealed, respecting God and his designs, and of idle legends of various kinds respecting wonder-working saints, which have disgraced the Romish Church. The sanction afforded to these, by persons who did not themselves believe them, is a fault referable to

[b] Essay IV. First Series.

another head, (to be mentioned subsequently,) as springing from a dishonest pursuit of the expedient rather than the true: but it is probable that the far greater part of such idle tales had not their *origin* in any deep and politic contrivance, but in men's natural passion for what is marvellous, and readiness to cater for that passion in each other;—in the universal fondness of the human mind for speculative knowledge respecting things curious and things hidden, rather than (what alone the Scriptures supply) practical knowledge respecting things which have a reference to our wants.

Equally natural to man, and closely connected, as will hereafter be shewn, with the error just mentioned, is the disposition to trust in *vicarious* worship and obedience—the desire and hope of transferring from one man to another the merit of good works, and the benefit of devotional exercises; so as to enable the mass of the people to serve God, as it were, by proxy. On this point I have elsewhere[c] offered some remarks,

---

[c] In the last of Five Discourses delivered before the University, and subsequently published.

(which are expanded and followed up in the present work,) with a view to shew that it is the main cause, rather than the consequence, of the whole Romish system of priestcraft; one of the great features of which is, the change of the very office of the Christian Priest, Πρεσβύτερος, into that of the Jewish or Pagan Priest, in the other sense of the word, answering to Ἱερεύς. I observed that the people were very easily deceived in this point, because they were eagerly craving for deception;—that the same disposition had manifested itself no less strongly among the Pagan nations;—and that the same tendency is, and ever will be, breaking out in one shape or another, among Protestants, and in every form of religion.

III. No less characteristic of the natural man, is, a vicious preference of supposed expediency, to truth; and a consequent readiness to employ false reasons for satisfying the minds of the people;—to connive at, or foster, supposed salutary or innocent delusions; whence arose the sanction given to all the monstrous train of pious frauds, legendary tales, and lying miracles, for which the Romish Church has been so justly stigmatized. And as it is notorious that the ancient lawgivers and philosophers encouraged (for political purposes) a belief in the mythological fables which they themselves *dis*believed, there can be no doubt that this disposition also is not to be attributed to the Church of Rome as its *cause*, but that *that* Church merely furnishes one set of instances of its *effects;* and that consequently an earnest watchfulness against those effects, is to be inculcated not merely on such as may be in danger of being misled into Romanism, but on every descendant of Adam.

IV. Again, no *one* perhaps of the errors of the Romish Church has exposed her to greater censure, or has been productive of more mischievous results, than the claim to infallibility;—the investing, without any sufficient grounds, weak and fallible men with an attribute of Deity. Now the ready acquiescence in such an extravagant claim (which never could have been maintained had not men been found thus ready to acquiesce in it) may easily be traced to the principles of our corrupt nature;—to that indolence in investigation, indifference about truth [d], and ready

---

[d] Ἀταλαίπωρος τοῖς πολλοῖς ἡ ζήτησις τῆς ἀληθείας, καὶ ἐπὶ τὰ ἕτοιμα μᾶλλον τρέπονται.

acquiescence in what is put before us, of which the Greek historian complained long before the Christian era; and to that dislike of suspense— and consequent willingness to make a short and final appeal to some authority which should be regarded as decisive, with a view to quash disputes, and save the labour of inquiry. That such a disposition is not at least peculiar to the votaries of the religion of Rome, or confined even to religious subjects, is evident, from the appeals of pretended students in philosophy to the decisions of Pythagoras, and subsequently of Aristotle, as precluding all further dispute or doubt. It is for Protestants therefore to remember, that they are not secured by the mere circumstance of their being such, from all danger of indulging this disposition. There is indeed no danger of their appealing to the *Church of Rome* as an infallible authority to put a stop to all discussion; but the removal of that particular danger, should only put us the more on our guard against the same fault (as it is a fault of our common nature) breaking out in some new shape.

V. One of the heaviest charges against the Romish Church may be added to those already alluded to—the spirit of Persecution; which is as far as any of her other enormities from being peculiar to that Church, or even to the case of religion: witness, among many other instances, the furious and bitter spirit shewn by the Nominalists and Realists in their contests concerning abstruse points of metaphysics. The Romish system did not properly introduce intolerance, but rather, it was intolerance that introduced and established the system of Romanism; and that (in another part of the world) no less successfully called in the sword for the establishment of Mahometism. So congenial indeed to " the natural Man" is the resort to force for the establishment of one system of doctrines and the suppression of another, that we find many of the Reformers, after they had clearly perceived nearly all the *other* errors in which they had been brought up, yet entertaining no doubt whatever as to the right, and the duty, of maintaining religious truth by coercive means.

VI. Another tendency, as conspicuous as those above mentioned in the Romish Church, and, like its other errors, by no means *confined* to that Church, is the confident security with which the

Catholics, as they call themselves, trust in that *name*, as denoting their being members of that sacred body, the only true Church, whose holy character and title to divine favour they seem to consider as a kind of common property, and a safeguard to all her members: even as the Jews of old " said within themselves, We are Abraham's children;" flattering themselves that on that ground, however little they might resemble Abraham in faith and in works, God would surely never cast them off. This error is manifestly common to the Romanists with those who put the same kind of trust in the *name* of Protestant or of Christian; and who regard their connection with a holy and richly-endowed community, rather as a substitute for personal holiness, than as a motive for aiming at a still higher degree of it, and a privilege involving a higher responsibility.

§. 4. In treating of all these points, I shall adhere to the plan hitherto pursued, viz. of contemplating the errors of the Romanists, not with a view to our own justification in withdrawing from their communion; nor again, for the sake of guarding against the danger of being seduced by their arguments, (important as these objects may be;) but with a view to what I cannot but regard as the much greater danger, of falling into corresponding errors to theirs—of being taken captive by the same temptations under different forms—of overlooking, in practice, the important truth, that the spirit of Romanism is substantially the spirit of Human Nature.

We are all of us in these days likely to hear and to read most copious discussions of the tenets and practices of the Church of Rome. Whatever may be the views of each of my readers respecting the political question which has chiefly given rise to these discussions, (a question which, like all others of a political character, I have always thought had better be waived in theological works,) I would suggest these reflections as profitable to be kept in view by all, while occupied with such discussions: how far we are pure from Romish errors in another shape;—from what quarters, and under what disguises, we are liable to be assailed by temptations, substantially, though not externally, the same with those which seduced into all her corruptions the Church of Rome; and which gradually changed her bridal purity for the accumulated defilements of "the mother of harlots;"—and how we may best guard against the spirit of Superstition, (of which, be it remembered, none, even the most superstitious, ever suspect themselves)—the spirit of Persecution—the spirit of insincerity, of Fraud, and of indifference to truth—in short, all those evil propensities which are fitly characterized in one word as, the spirit of Romanism. All these dangers, as they did not *begin* with the Romish system, cannot be expected to end with it: they emanate not from that corrupt Church alone, but from the corruption of our common nature; and none consequently are more open to them, than those who are disposed to think themselves secured by merely keeping out of the pale of that Church, and inveighing against her enormities.

Such a false security indeed is itself one of the worst of the Romish errors; that of mistaking *names* for things, and trusting in a specious *title*, without enquiring how far we possess the character which that title implies. "He is not a Jew," says Paul, "who is one outwardly, neither is that circumcision which is outward in the flesh; but he is a Jew who is one inwardly; and circumcision is that of the heart, in the spirit and not in the letter; whose praise is not of men, but of God." It is for us therefore ever to remember, for thus only can we turn to account the apostle's admonition, that as that man was not, in the sight of God, a Jew, to any profitable purpose for himself, but rather to his aggravated condemnation, who was only outwardly a Jew; so neither, by parity of reasoning, is he in God's sight a Christian—a " Catholic Christian"—a " Protestant"—a " Reformed" Christian—who is one outwardly; but he who is reformed inwardly —whose heart is Christian—and who protests not with his lips only, but in his life—" in the spirit and not in the letter"—against such depravation of Gospel-truth, and departure from Gospel-holiness, as he censures in his erring brethren.

§. 5. In treating of superstitious worship, the point at present more immediately before us, it is worth remarking, that (as indeed has been already hinted) many of the Romanist-practices bear a strong resemblance to those of the idolatrous Israelites. In particular, their veneration for the wood of the supposed true Cross, has a correspondence approaching to identity, with the veneration of the Israelites for the brazen serpent which Hezekiah destroyed; only that the more ancient superstition was one degree less irrational; inasmuch as the image was that which had itself been a more immediate instrument of a miraculous deliverance; whereas what typically corresponds to it in the Christian dispensation, is (as our Lord himself points out) not the cross on which He suffered, but the very person of the suffering Redeemer.

The Romanists, in paying a *slavish* worship (it is *their own* expression, δουλεία) not only to images and relics, but also to saints, are guilty of *both* those kinds of superstition, the unsparing suppression of *both* of which, constitutes the distinguished and peculiar merit of that upright and zealous prince, Hezekiah. He was not satisfied, like many other kings, with putting down that branch of superstition which involves the breach of the first Commandment—the setting up of false gods; but was equally decisive in his reprobation of the other branch also—the worship of the true God by the medium of prohibited emblems, and with unauthorized and superstitious rites. Of these two kinds of superstition, the latter is continually liable, in practice, to slide into the former, by such insensible degrees, that it is often hard to decide, in particular cases, *where* the breach of the second Commandment ends, and that of the first begins. The distinction is not however for that reason useless; perhaps it is even the more useful on that very account, and was for that reason preserved, in those two Commandments; of which the second serves as a kind of outwork to the first, to guard against all gradual *approaches* to a violation of it—to keep men at a *distance* from the danger of infringing the majesty of the jealous God.

Accordingly, besides the numerous warnings which Moses gives the Israelites against being seduced into worshipping the false gods of the nations of Canaan, he also cautions them, not to imitate in their worship of the Lord, the superstitious rites used by the heathen in the service of *their* deities. They are forbidden to inquire, "How did these nations serve their gods?" and to say, " Even so will I do likewise. Thou shalt not do so unto the Lord thy God."

Both injunctions the Israelites frequently violated; many of them, while they observed the first Commandment in abstaining from the worship of Baal and the other gods of the heathen, infringing nevertheless the second, by their use of images: of which we have an instance in the case of Jeroboam "who made Israel to sin;" the golden calves which he set up being clearly designed as emblematical representations of the true God: for he said, "These be thy gods, O Israel, which *brought thee out of the land of Egypt*." This was emphatically called "the sin of Jeroboam;" and the distinction above alluded to is noticed in the case (to omit numberless others) of Jehu; "thus Jehu destroyed Baal out of Israel: howbeit from the sins of Jeroboam the son of Nebat, who made Israel to sin, Jehu departed not from after them, to wit, the golden calves that were in Bethel, and that were in Dan."

And we find also numerous instances (besides this direct violation of the second Commandment) of the introduction of unauthorized and superstitious rites in the worship of the true God.

This two-fold division of Superstition I have the more strongly dwelt on, both because it is frequently overlooked, and because inattention to it is likely to lead to dangerous consequences.

I would not however be understood as contending for any arbitrary and unusual signification of the word; but I conceive, that by Superstition is commonly understood, not, as a popular though superficial writer has defined it, "an excess of religion," (at least in the ordinary sense of the word *excess*,) as if any one *could* have *too much* of true religion, but, any *misdirection* of religious feeling; manifested either in shewing religious veneration or regard to objects which deserve *none*; i. e. properly speaking, the worship of false gods; or, in the assignment of such a degree, or such a kind of religious veneration to any object, as that object, though worthy of some reverence, does not deserve; or in the worship of the true God through the medium of improper ceremonies or symbols.

This latter branch of superstition is extremely liable, as I have already remarked, to degenerate insensibly into the former. The Israelite, e. g. who was accustomed to worship Jehovah through the medium of a sensible image, would be very likely, in time, to transfer a larger and larger portion of his adoration to the image itself; and in proportion as he annexed to it any idea of especial sanctity, he would be, insensibly, more and more falling into the error of adoring an image, in the only sense in which it is conceivable that an image *can* be adored.

In avowing my conviction that this is the case with a large proportion of the members of the Romish Church, and that they are consequently most decidedly chargeable with the sin of Idolatry, I am aware that I run counter to the opinions (I might rather perhaps say to the expressions) of some enlightened Protestants. But these, I conceive, are not so much mistaken in their judgment, as inaccurate in their language. It is said, e. g. that when the Romanists offer up their prayers before a crucifix, or before a piece of bread, they do not design to worship a piece of wood or a piece of bread, as such, but our Lord

Jesus Christ as represented by the one, and as actually present in the other. And certainly, if they intend to direct their worship to the one true God, they are not guilty of a breach of the *first* Commandment; but this does not clear them of the charge of infringing the second; they may be guilty of superstition, though not of every kind and degree of superstition: and if the practices, I have alluded to, do not constitute that kind of superstition which is properly called idolatry, let us be allowed to inquire, what does? Will it be said that idolatry consists in worshipping a piece of wood as *such*—as a mere piece of wood? I would ask in reply, Who then ever was, or can be, guilty of it? The thing is not only practically impossible, but is inconceivable, and a contradiction in terms. The most gross-minded Israelite that ever offered up his prayers before a golden calf, implied, by that very act, his belief that it was something more than a mere piece of gold, and that there resided in it a certain divine intelligence. The argument therefore is not so much a vindication of any party from the charge of idolatry, as, a vindication of idolatry itself.

It has been said, I believe, by some Protestants,

respecting the alleged idolatry of adoring the sacred elements at the Eucharist, " it *would* be idolatrous, if *I* were to join in it :" if this means, " supposing you to have the same belief in transubstantiation that the Romanists have," this is only a circuitous mode of saying that they are idolaters; but if it means, " were you to join in it, supposing you to have the Protestant belief that the consecrated bread is merely bread," the supposition involves an absurdity and self-contradiction. A man may indeed *feign*, and outwardly indicate, in order to deceive his fellow-man, an adoration of what he believes to be merely a piece of bread or of wood ; but that he should really and inwardly adore, what he believes at the moment to be no more than mere bread or mere wood, is not only impossible, but absolutely unmeaning, being at variance with the very notion of adoration.

If therefore a Romanist adores the true God under the form of bread [e], which he holds to be

[e] For the Romish doctrine is, as Mr. Blanco White has plainly shewn, not, as they themselves declare, that bread is transformed into the body of Christ, but that *Christ is transformed into bread*, in the sense which the words according to invariable usage convey.

the real literal body of Christ, or if, in worshipping before a crucifix, he attributes a certain sanctity to the image, as if some divine virtue were actually present in it, (and that this is done is plain from the preference shewn of one image to another,) he is clearly as much guilty of idolatry as the Israelites in worshipping the golden calf and the brazen serpent: it being thus only, that any one *can* practise idolatry.

In making this declaration, however, it is not my object either to lead Protestants to exult uncharitably over their erring brethren, or to vindicate our own renunciation of their errors; but rather to point out the danger which must ever beset all of us, of falling into similar errors in another shape, and under other names; for ten thousand of the greatest faults in our neighbour are of less consequence to *us*, than one, of the smallest, in ourselves.

The Israelites of old were warned not only to worship none of the gods of the heathen, but to copy none of their superstitions; "Ye shall not do so to the Lord your God." Now *they* probably were disposed to think themselves secure from the danger of corrupting their own religion, in their deep abhorrence of the religions of those nations whom the Lord had cast out before them. The Church of Rome, again, thought itself safe from superstition, by its rejection of those particular superstitions of which the Israelites and the Pagans were guilty. And Protestants, again, are no less disposed to feel the same security, on account of their abhorrence of the particular superstitions of the Romanists. The images used by the Papists are not the same with those for worshipping which the Israelites were condemned: and they again doubtless pleaded that the golden calves and the brazen serpent were not the idols of the Canaanites; and thus does each successive generation censure the faults and follies of the preceding, without taking sufficient heed to itself, or recognizing, as they arise, errors substantially the same, though under new shapes.

The superstitious and the other errors of the Romanists were, as I have already observed, not the result of systematic contrivance, but sprung up spontaneously as the indigenous growth of the human heart: they arose successively, gradually, and imperceptibly; and were in most instances, probably, first overlooked, then tolerated, and then sanctioned, and finally embodied in that detestable system, of which they are rather to be regarded as the cause than the effect. Since then, as I have said, corruptions of religion neither first sprang from Romanism, nor can be expected to end with it, the tendency to them being inherent in our common nature; it is evident that constant watchfulness alone can preserve us from, not the very same, corruptions with those of our predecessors, but, similar ones under some fresh disguise; and that this danger is enhanced by the very circumstance which seems to secure us from it—our abhorrence of those errors in them. From practices the very same in name and form with theirs, such abhorrence is indeed a safeguard; while at the same time it makes us the less ready to suspect ourselves of the faults disguised: the vain security thus generated, draws off our thoughts from self-examination; a task for which the mind is in general least fitted, when it is most occupied in detecting and exposing the faults of others. In treating then of such corruptions of religion as those into which the Church of Rome has fallen, my primary object is to excite a spirit not of self-congratulation and self-confidence, but of self-distrust and self-examination.

§. 6. With respect to that particular class of corruptions now before us, which comes under the general title of Superstition, it is requisite (though it is somewhat strange that it should be so) to premise a remark on the *enormity* of the evil in question. The mischiefs of Superstition are, I conceive, much underrated. It is by many regarded, not as any sin, but as a mere harmless folly, at the worst;—as, in some instances, an amiable weakness, or even a salutary delusion. Its votaries are pitied, as in some cases subjected to needless and painful restraints, and undergoing groundless terrors;—sometimes they are ridiculed as enslaved to absurd and puerile observances: but whether pitied or laughed at, superstitious Christians are often regarded as likely, at least as not the *less* likely on account of their superstition, to have secured the essentials of religion;—as believing and practising what is needful towards salvation, and as only carrying their faith and their practice unnecessarily and unreasonably to the point of weak credulity and foolish scrupulosity. This view of the subject has a strong tendency to confirm the superstitious, and even to add to their number. They feel that if there is any doubt, they are surely on the *safe* side. " Supposing I am in error on this or that point," (a man may say,) "I am merely doing something superfluous; at the worst I suffer some temporary inconvenience, and perhaps have to encounter some ridicule; but if the error be on the other side, I risk my salvation by embracing it; my present course therefore is evidently the safest."

What force this argument has in the hands of the Romanists, I need hardly remind my readers. Of converts to Romanism probably three out of four, especially of the ignorant and the weak-minded, have been drawn over, in the first instance at least, by the consideration, that that is the *safe* side [f].

[f] "The Romanists in general, but more especially those who, in the midst of doubt, are anxious to save themselves from the painful step of changing their communion, comfort themselves with the idea, that after all *Roman Catholics are on the safe side*. If Protestants should be saved, they themselves have made "assurance double sure:" if Protestantism be Christianity, Romanists have it all, and a great deal besides.

With the danger however of being seduced into the pale of the Romish Church, I am not at present concerned, but with the danger of Superstition generally. In speaking of that point,

" I know of few absurdities that can be compared to this. Let me make it clear to you by a familiar example. Suppose a poor, helpless person is dying of a dreadful complaint. An eminent physician hears of his distress; calls on him, and prepares a medicine, which he desires the patient to take, under a strong injunction to trust in it alone for life. In the absence of the physician, our patient begins to think on the prescription, and because it appears to him too simple, mixes it with every quack medicine that the neighbours recommend. Having swallowed the whole, he now comforts himself with the assurance that he is on the safe side. Why? because he has mistrusted the physician, and divided his confidence between the only man whose skill can save him, and the old women of the village.

" O foolish Galatians!" (I am irresistibly impelled to exclaim with St. Paul,) " who hath bewitched you, that ye should not obey the truth?" O blind and deluded people! how can you imagine that the eternal life promised to faith in Christ will be doubly secured by shewing and proving your mistrust, through the use of the fanciful ways of pleasing God, invented and set forth by Rome?" *Blanco White's Letter to Converts from Romanism.* This excellent little tract is less known than it deserves.

as well as (hereafter) of others, connected with the *spirit* of Romanism, I wish to be understood as not calling for harsh censure on individuals, but only on offences as they are in themselves. How far the superstition of any individual may be excusable or blamable in the sight of God, can be pronounced by Him alone, who alone is able to estimate each man's strength or weakness, his opportunities of gaining knowledge, and his employment or neglect of those opportunities. But the same may be said of every other offence, as well as of the one in question. Of Superstition itself in all its various forms and degrees, I cannot think otherwise than that it is not merely a folly to be ridiculed, but a mischief to be dreaded; and that its tendency is, in most cases, as far as it extends, destructive of true piety.

The disposition to reverence some superhuman Power, and in some way or other to endeavour to recommend ourselves to the favour of that Power, is (more or less in different individuals) a natural and original sentiment of the human mind. The great Enemy of Man finds it easier in most cases to misdirect, than to eradicate this. If an exercise for this religious sentiment can be provided—

if this natural craving after divine worship (if I may so speak) can be satisfied—by the practice of superstitious ceremonies, true piety will be much more easily extinguished ;—the conscience will on this point have been set at rest ;—God's place in the heart will, as it were, have been pre-occupied by an idol ; and that genuine religion which consists in a devotedness of the affections to God, operating in the improvement of the moral character, will be more effectually shut out, from the religious feelings of our nature having found another vent, and exhausted themselves on vanities of man's devising.

To illustrate as fully as might be done this debasing and corrupting tendency of Superstition, by an examination of the numberless instances of it which might but too readily be found, would far exceed my limits, and would be, to most of my readers, in a great degree unnecessary. But I cannot omit, in confirmation of what has been said, one general remark, which is applicable to most of these instances : that one of the most prevailing characteristics of Superstition, at least which is found more or less in most species of it, is, the attributing of some sacred efficacy to the performance of an *outward act*, or the presence of some *material object*, without any inward devotion of the heart being required to accompany it;—without, in short, any thing else being needed, except, in some cases, an undoubting faith in that intrinsic efficacy. The tendency thus to disjoin religious observances (i. e. what are *intended* to be such) from heartfelt and practical religion, is one of the most besetting evils of our corrupt nature; and it is the very root of most superstitions. Now no one can fail to perceive how opposite this is to true piety.

Empty forms not only supersede piety by standing in its place, but gradually alter the habits of the mind, and render it unfit for the exercise of genuine pious sentiment. Even the natural food of religion (if I may so speak) is thus converted into its poison.

Our very prayers, for example, and our perusal of the holy Scriptures, become superstitious, in proportion as any one expects them to operate as a charm—attributing efficacy to the mere words, while his feelings and thoughts are not occupied in what he is doing.

Every religious ceremony or exercise, however well calculated, in itself, to improve the heart, is liable, as I have said, thus to degenerate into a mere form, and consequently to become superstitious; but in proportion as the outward observances are the more complex and operose, and the more unmeaning or unintelligible, the more danger is there of superstitiously attaching a sort of magical efficacy to the bare outward act, independent of mental devotion. If, for example, even our prayers are liable, without constant watchfulness, to become a superstitious form, by our " honouring God with our lips, while our heart is far from Him," this result is almost unavoidable when the prayers are recited in an unknown tongue, and with a prescribed number of vain repetitions, crossings, and telling of beads. And men of a timorous mind, having once taken up a wrong notion of what religion consists in, seek a refuge from doubt and anxiety, a substitute for inward piety, and, too often, a compensation for an evil life, in an endless multiplication of superstitious observances;—of pilgrimages, sprinklings with holy water, veneration of relics, and the like. And hence the enormous accumulation of superstitions, which, in the course of many centuries, gradually arose in the Romish and Greek Churches.

§. 7. And it is a circumstance not a little remarkable, that, in many instances at least, Superstition not only does not promote true Religion, but even tends to generate *Profaneness;* and that, not merely in other points, but even in respect of the very objects of the superstitious reverence. In proof of this I can cite the testimony of an eminently competent witness, as far at least as one Roman-Catholic country (Spain) is concerned; the Author, after having mentioned the extravagant and absurd superstitions of the ceremonies which take place on Good Friday, adds, " I have carefully glided over such parts of this absurd performance as would shock many an English reader, even in narrative. Yet such is the strange mixture of superstition and profaneness in the people for whose gratification these scenes are exhibited, that though any attempt to expose the indecency of these shows would rouse their zeal " to the knife," I cannot venture to translate the jokes and sallies of wit that are frequently heard among the Spanish peasantry upon these sacred topics[g]." The like strange mixture is found in other Roman-Catholic and also in Pagan countries; particularly among the Hindoos, who are described as habitually reviling their gods in the grossest terms, on the occasion of any untoward event.

In this country a large proportion of the superstition that exists, is connected more or less with the agency of evil spirits; and accordingly (in conformity with the strange principle of our nature just mentioned) nothing is so common a theme of profane jests among the vulgar of all ranks, as the Devil, and every thing relating to that Being, including the "everlasting fire prepared for him and his angels;" and this, by no means exclusively, or chiefly, among such as disbelieve what Scripture says on the subject; but, on the contrary, even the most, among those who give credit to a multitude of legendary tales also, quite unwarranted by Scripture.

This curious anomaly may perhaps be, in a great measure at least, accounted for, from the consideration, that as Superstition imposes a yoke

[g] Doblado's Letters from Spain, p. 264.

rather of fear than of love, her votaries are glad to *take revenge*, as it were, when galled by this yoke, and to indemnify themselves in some degree both for the irksomeness of their restraints and tasks, and also for the *degradation*, (some sense of which is always excited by a consciousness of slavish dread,) by taking liberties, *wherever they dare*, either in the way of insult or of playfulness, with the objects of their dread. And jests on sacred subjects, it is well known, are, when men are so disposed, the most easily produced of any; because the *contrast* between a dignified and a low image, exhibited in combination, (in which the whole force of the ludicrous consists,) is in this case the most striking[h].

[h] It is commonly said, that there is no wit in profane jests; but it would be hard to frame any definition of wit that should exclude them. It would be more correct to say, (and I believe that is what is really meant,) that the practice displays *no great powers* of wit, because the subject-matter renders it so particularly easy; and that (for the very same reason) it affords the least gratification (apart from all higher considerations) to judges of good taste; for a great part of the pleasure afforded by wit results from a *perception* of *skill* displayed, and *difficulty* surmounted.

But how comes it that they ever do *dare*, as we see is the fact, to take these liberties? Another characteristic of Superstition will perhaps explain this also. It is, as I have just said, characteristic of Superstition to enjoin, and to attribute efficacy to, the mere performance of some specific outward acts—the use of some material object, without any loyal affectionate devotion of heart being required to accompany such acts, and to pervade the whole life as a ruling motive. Hence, the rigid observance of the precise directions given, leaves the votary secure, at ease in conscience, and at liberty, as well as in a disposition, to indulge in profaneness. In like manner a patient, who dares not refuse to swallow a nauseous dose and to confine himself to a strict regimen, yet is both vexed and somewhat ashamed of submitting to the annoyance, will sometimes take his revenge, as it were, by abusive ridicule of his medical attendant and his drugs; knowing that this will not, so long as he does but take the medicines, diminish their efficacy. Superstitious observances are a kind of distasteful or disgusting remedy, which however is to operate if it be but swallowed; and on which accordingly the votary sometimes ventures gladly to revenge himself.

The more ready therefore in any instance the superstitions of the Romish Church approached to, and blended themselves with, true religion, the more did they deteriorate the spirit of it;—the more did the poisonous parasite, twining round the fairest boughs of the good tree, blight by its noxious neighbourhood the fruits which that should have borne.

We cannot indeed be too thankful to God, that by his blessing, our ancestors perceived and undertook to reform these abuses: but my especial object in now adverting to the errors of the Romanists is, to call your attention to this important consideration; that such a multitude and variety of superstitions, as troublesome as they are absurd, never could have been introduced by any devices of priestcraft, had there not been in the human mind that strong natural *tendency* to Superstition which has just been described. And this being the case—this tendency being, as it is, a part of our common nature, it is for us to guard against the danger in ourselves, instead of exulting in a vain confidence that we are exempt and safe from it. The things we ought to learn, and to learn with a view to our own profit, from the example of the Romish Church, are, the mischievous effects of Superstition, and, Man's proneness to it.

That Superstition does exist, to no inconsiderable extent, in Protestant countries, which is what the foregoing reasonings, even independently of experience, would prepare us to expect, few, I imagine, would venture to deny; though perhaps fewer still are fully aware of its amount, or sufficiently on their guard against the danger.

§. 8. With respect to the particular points on which Superstition is most to be dreaded, and towards which, consequently, our vigilance should be especially directed, I am precluded by several considerations from entering on any detailed examination.

The enumeration of all, or nearly all, the superstitions which either actually exist, or are likely to arise, would far exceed my purposed limits. And I am sensible that to advert even to a few of these, is likely to be less profitable than I could wish; inasmuch as the same remarks will usually be a superfluous truism to one person, and a revolting paradox to another. For any one who practises, or tolerates and approves, any superstition, is of course not accustomed (at least should in charity not be presumed to be accustomed) to consider it as superstition, nor would be prepared to admit the censure without detailed argument and calm consideration; while one who *does* regard it as superstitious, has himself already pronounced that censure.

To this must be added, that in most instances the very same thing will be superstitious to some persons, and not to others. The adoration of saints indeed, or of any other Being besides the one true God, must be always, and in itself, superstitious: but in the great majority of instances, the very same outward rites, and sensible objects, may be either a help to devotion, or a substitute for it; such as sacred music—the repetition of prayers—the assembling in edifices set apart for divine worship—the assuming of certain bodily postures, &c. In all such cases, the religion or the superstition exist in the mind of the person, and are only incidentally connected with the external objects and observances. Of these last, the *best* that can be said of any of them is, that they are well *calculated* to cherish feelings of rational devotion: the *worst* that can be said of any of them is, that they are peculiarly *liable* to become superstitious. But even pictures and images are not in themselves superstitious; and accordingly we do not now exclude them from our houses of worship; though if we found them now liable to any of that abuse which has grown to such an enormous height among the Romanists, it would be our duty to treat them as Hezekiah did the brazen serpent, which "he brake in pieces, because the Israelites burnt incense to it." And, on the other hand, there is no act or object connected with divine worship which may not *become* superstitious, through the worshipper's trusting in the efficacy of outward forms, while his heart is far from God. Our reformers, therefore, shewed their discretion in their assertion respecting the Liturgy and forms of Ordination which they drew up, that these "contained nothing *in itself* superstitious:" they knew by sad experience that nothing but the worshipper's vigilant self-examination can secure either human or divine ordinances from *becoming* (to him) superstitious.

What has been said may be sufficient to shew, that this vigilant examination and caution against superstition on each particular point, must be practised by each person for himself, both with a view to his own conduct, and that of all those who may be more especially under his care; and that the necessity of this cannot be superseded by any general description.

Enough also has been said, I trust, to shew both the vast importance of this vigilant examination, and also the principles on which it should be conducted. I will notice however a few, and only a few, of those practices and notions, to which, as it seems to me, especial attention should be directed, as either savouring of Superstition, or peculiarly liable to lead to it. Several of my observations, I have no doubt, will appear utterly superfluous, to many of those among my readers who have not (not to those who have) been occupied diligently in the case of a parish, and in that essential part of it, frequent and confidential intercourse with all, and especially with the more unenlightened classes, of the parishioners. I pledge myself however to state nothing on the ground of mere conjecture—nothing which I have not been enabled fully to verify.

§. 9. I. That there exists among Protestants much of that branch of Romish superstition—the pretension to miraculous powers, or belief in miraculous occurrences, on slight grounds, no soberminded person, who is not quite ignorant of the existing state of things, can doubt[i]. We have among us pretenders to inspiration; some using that very term, and others virtually im-

---

[i] It would not be suitable to my present purpose, to enter on a minute inquiry into the use of several words connected with the present subject; but it may be worth while to remark, that, according to the most prevailing usage, " Fanaticism" implies Superstition, (i. e. " misdirected religious feeling,") but is not necessarily implied by it. If on very insufficient grounds I believe *another* person to be inspired, or any other miracle to have taken place, I am merely *superstitious;* if I thus believe *myself* to be inspired, or gifted with miraculous powers, I am also *fanatical.*

Enthusiasm seems to be employed as a more comprehensive term than Fanaticism, both as being sometimes used in a good, at least, a milder, sense, and also as extending to other things besides Religion.

plying as much: and we have many who see special "judgments" or other "interpositions" of Providence, in almost every remarkable, and in many of the most ordinary occurrences. Sometimes they apply to these the very term "miraculous;" sometimes they call them, which amounts to the very same, "providential;" for though it is literally true that nothing takes place which is not, in some sense, providential, it is plain for that very reason, that whatever is rightly *characterised* as providential, i. e. as *more* providential than other events, is properly miraculous[k].

If either Romanists, or any others, will give *sufficient proof* of the occurrence of a miracle, they ought to be listened to: but to pretend to, or to believe in, any miracle *without* sufficient proof, is clearly superstitious, whatever may be the system such a miracle is adduced to support.

[k] I ought in justice to say, that I believe many ephemeral writers, and careless talkers, occasionally use the words "providential," and "miraculous," (as well as many others,) without attaching any precise notion to them. They have been used to hear the words applied to *remarkable* occurrences; and from mere force of imitation do the same, as if the words were merely synonymous with "remarkable."

Most deeply is it to be regretted, that some writers, who have argued justly and forcibly against the error of looking for inspiration or other miraculous interferences, should have more than nullified the benefit done, by going on to explain away all that Scripture teaches respecting spiritual influence. Besides the danger, that they may propagate this error by means of the truth they have mixed up with it, there is also an opposite evil even much more to be apprehended; that the fanatics thus opposed may join with their opponents in representing the whole doctrine of grace as inseparably connected with their scheme of miraculous interferences and sensible inspiration; so that the whole must stand or fall together; and that they may then triumphantly urge, " See what violence one is driven to do to Scripture, and how much at variance he becomes with the Church of England, whenever he attempts to oppose our doctrine!" Too much care cannot be taken to testify *simultaneously* against both of these opposite errors.

II. Again, more Superstition exists than some persons are aware of, in relation to the Eucharist, and to the sacred " elements" (as they are still called[1]) which are administered in that rite. Several among the uneducated (and some even among the higher) classes, and those of them not least who never partake[m], or design to partake, of the holy Communion till they believe themselves on the bed of death, have a strong faith in the efficacy, as a medicine, of what they call " Sacrament-wine ;" i. e. wine which either has been, or is designed to be, (for they know too little of the rite to distinguish between the two,) *consecrated* for this use. They have been known to apply for it to the minister as an infallible cure for some particular diseases of children :—confidently asserting (indeed the very existence and continuance of the superstition forbids us to hope that such applications have always been made *in vain*) that they have formerly obtained it for that use. Others have

[1] Agreeably to the language of the Schoolmen; who framed the doctrine of Transubstantiation, as it now stands, so completely from Aristotle's writings, that it never could have existed in any thing like its present form, had that Philosopher not been studied.

[m] This is one instance out of a multitude, in which Superstition, instead of promoting, as some persons vainly imagine, true Religion, stands in the place of it.

been known, when attending at the Lord's Table, to secrete, for the purpose of carrying home, a portion of the consecrated bread handed to them; doubtless with a view to some similar superstitious use [n]. Others again, above the very poorest class, have been known to petition for a portion of the " Sacrament-money," i. e. the alms then collected, (offering to purchase it for the same sum in other pieces of money,) to be forged into a ring as an infallible cure for fits. This again is a superstition which could hardly have maintained its ground, if it had never been on any occasion indulged by those whose office is to repress it.

[n] I have detected and stopped this practice among those who are called to consume the remainder of the bread and wine after the close of the Service. Let me be permitted to call the attention of officiating ministers to the Rubric, and to recommend a strict adherence to it, in what relates to this matter: " if any remain of that which was consecrated, it shall not be carried out of the church, but the priest and such other of the communicants as he shall then *call unto him*, shall, immediately after the Blessing, reverently eat and drink the same:" i. e. the communicants (as it must be understood) *remaining* in the minister's presence, into which he had " called" them.

Too common again, and well known, is the case of persons who have, during the hours of health, systematically abstained from communicating, and who have pleaded, among other excuses, with great truth, their *ignorance*, while they have refused to listen to the offered instruction—of these same persons when on their deathbed, though conscious of the *same ignorance* respecting the whole nature and design of the ceremony, and in no condition then to learn°, yet

---

° Sometimes without any *wish*, even then, for previous instruction; or, consequently, any notion that the benefit of the Sacrament is at all dependent on a knowledge of our Religion. "Do pray, dear Sir, give me the Sacrament first, and then talk as much as you please," is an answer by which I have known a sick man perseveringly repel the attempts of the minister to examine into the state of his mind, and to impart to him the requisite instruction.

As for the point of *sincerity* or *insincerity*, no one of course, except the Searcher of hearts, can be sure in every instance, whether an individual is, or is not, in this respect, a fit communicant: we have only to receive his solemn professions; and our admitting him on the strength of these, does not, supposing them to be in fact hypocritical, give any countenance to the superstitious belief, that an insincere communicant derives benefit from the rite: since we admit him on the supposition of his being *not* insincere; but it is otherwise in

earnestly craving the administration of this sacrament, and trusting (while their surrounding friends cherish their confidence) that the words repeated, and the bodily act of receiving the bread and wine, will operate as a charm to ensure salvation, like the " extreme unction" of the Romanists. Now if this is not a superstitious abuse of the ordinance, what is?

III. Nor has the other sacrament escaped the defilement of Superstition. Not a few there are who eagerly seek it with as superstitious a reverence as that with which they shrink from the Lord's Supper, and with, if possible, a still more complete ignorance of its nature. They seem to regard the giving of a *name*[p] to an infant as the

respect of the point of *knowledge* or ignorance; *that* the minister *can* ascertain; and if he neglect to do so, and to proceed accordingly, he is manifestly fostering Superstition.

[p] In a parish which had been grossly neglected under a former incumbent, the rite of Baptism was administered to several who had grown up without it: among the applicants was a young woman, who, it came out, had been already baptized, and who gave as a reason for applying, that she was dissatisfied with the *name* that had been given her, and wished for another.

most essential, or one of the most essential parts of the rite: understanding by the terms "Baptism" or "Christening," the public reception in church, (about which they are frequently very indifferent,) and knowing private Baptism by no other appellation than "Naming." And many are anxious that the ceremony should take place (I speak advisedly) if the child is very ill, in hopes that it may save his life; at all events, with strong expectation of some benefit, while yet they have no thought or intention of bringing him up with any kind of religious instruction and training; nor indeed have themselves either any religious knowledge, or any wish to gain it. To disjoin thus the means of grace from the fruits of grace—the expected benefit of the ordinance which admits a member into the Christian Church, from his care to lead a Christian life—is to convert a sacrament into a charm, and to "make the things that should have been for their health, be unto them an occasion of falling." There is no need to expatiate on the mischievous absurdity of such notions and such conduct, or (to those at least of my readers who have been engaged in the care of large parishes) on their prevalence. The point to which it is my present object to call attention, is, the *superstition* involved in them; which bears but too close a resemblance to those of the Church of Rome relative to the same sacrament [q].

Among the many evils to be traced to this particular superstition, is to be reckoned I think, in a great degree, the prevalence (among many of our own Clergy) of a system of doctrine which

---

[q] The present instance illustrates but too well what has been above said respecting the connexion between Superstition and Profaneness. Both exist in a remarkable degree in relation to the sacrament of Baptism. Few of my readers, I fear, will need more than to be merely reminded of the light and irreverent application of the term "christening," on any occasion of giving "a name" to any thing. Now if there be any thing intrinsically reasonable in the third Commandment, it surely is applicable, in its spirit, not merely to the name of God, but also to all the terms appropriated to his ordinances; in short, to all the language denoting any thing sacred. But in the present case, there exists a more palpable, more deliberate, and more revolting kind of profaneness, in the solemn mockery of what is called "christening a ship;" in which the sacrament itself, not the mere name of it, is regularly, formally, and with obtrusive pomp, "taken in vain," to the secret scorn and triumph of infidels, and to the disgrace of a nation calling itself Christian and Protestant.

goes to disjoin completely from "the outward visible sign of baptism" all "inward spiritual grace:" and likewise the continuance and increase of the Anabaptist-system; which indeed the doctrine just alluded to tends greatly to foster. An attentive hearer of one of these divines, taught to regard his own baptism as hardly more than an empty form, is throughly prepared to become a convert to the first Anabaptist he meets with[r].

IV. It is not perhaps generally known, how much Superstition prevails in respect of the repetition of Prayers. Protestants are accustomed to censure, as one of the most flagrant of Romish corruptions, the use of prayers in an unknown tongue: and it is plain that it makes no practical difference to the individual whether the words he utters are Latin or English, so long as they convey no sense to his mind. Now the practice of reciting unmeaning prayers (unmeaning, that is, to the person using them) prevails to a greater extent than perhaps many persons are aware. Many probably do not even know that there are invocations to angels and

[r] See Essay IX. second Series, p. 323—6.

to the four Evangelists, (which it is to be *hoped* are not at all understood,) in use at the present day in the devotions of some among the more ignorant classes of professed Protestants. I know that the caution given in Dr. Hawkins's excellent " Manual for Christians after Confirmation," (ch. v. §. 1.) that " to repeat the *creed* is not to *pray*," startled some persons as being manifestly needless. But the fact bears him out. The practice is by no means uncommon of reciting the Apostle's Creed as a portion of prayer. Now it is manifest that whoever makes such a mistake, might just as well recite it in Latin as in English; since it is plain he cannot understand even the general sense and drift of it. And it is equally manifest that the case would not be at all altered, if the formula he recited really *were* a prayer; since it would be an evident superstition to attach any spiritual virtue to the mere utterance by rote, in whatever language, of words, however in themselves appropriate.

And this leads me to remark, that the practice of teaching or allowing very young children to learn by heart ⁸ prayers, psalms, portions of Scripture, &c. which they are incapable at the

⁸ "It need hardly be observed how important it is, with a view to these objects, to abstain carefully from the practice, still too prevalent, though much less so, we believe, than formerly, of compelling, or encouraging, or even allowing, children to learn by rote forms of prayer, catechisms, hymns, or in short any thing connected with morality and religion, when they attach no meaning to the words they utter. It is done on the plea that they will hereafter learn the meaning of what they have been thus taught, and will be able to make a practical use of it. But no attempt at economy of time can be more injudicious. Let any child whose capacity is so far matured as to enable him to comprehend an explanation, e. g. of the Lord's Prayer, have it *then* put before him for the first time, and when he is made acquainted with the meaning of it, set to learn it by heart; and can any one doubt that in less than half a day's application he would be able to repeat it fluently? And the same would be the case with other forms. All that is thus learned by rote by a child before he is competent to attach a meaning to the words he utters, would not, if all put together, amount to so much as would cost him, when able to understand it, a week's labour to learn perfectly. Whereas it may cost the toil, often the vain toil, of many years, to unlearn the habit of *formalism*—of repeating words by rote without attending to their meaning; a habit which

time, of understanding, is one which is very often superstitious, and almost always leads to

every one conversant with education knows to be in all subjects most readily acquired by children, and with difficulty avoided even with the utmost care of the teacher; but which such a plan must inevitably tend to generate. It is often said, and very truly, that it is important to form early habits of piety; but to train a child in one kind of habit, is not the most likely way of forming the opposite one: and nothing can be more contrary to true piety, than the Popish superstition (for such in fact it is) of attaching efficacy to the repetition of a certain form of words, as of a charm, independent of the understanding and of the heart.

"It is also said, with equal truth, that we ought to take advantage of the facility which children possess of learning words: but to infer from thence, that Providence designs us to make such a use (or rather abuse) of this gift as we have been censuring, is as if we were to take advantage of the readiness with which a new born babe swallows whatever is put into its mouth, to dose it with ardent spirits, instead of wholesome food and necessary medicine. The readiness with which children learn and remember words, is in truth a most important advantage if rightly employed; viz if applied to the acquiring that mass of what may be called *arbitrary* knowledge of insulated facts, which *can only* be learned by rote, and which is necessary in after life; when the acquisition of it would both be more troublesome, and would

superstition. I say "often" superstitious, because it is not necessarily so. Some teachers make their children commit these things to memory, merely as an exercise of memory, or in order that they may know the words against the time when they shall become competent to understand them, without giving the children any notion, that in repeating these words they are performing a devotional act[t]. There is nothing superstitious in this; though I cannot but think it a most injudicious practice, inasmuch as it involves a great risk of most

encroach on time that might otherwise be better employed. Chronology, names of countries, weights and measures, and indeed all the *words* of any language, are of this description. If a child had even ten times the ordinary degree of the faculty in question, a judicious teacher would find abundance of useful employment for it, without resorting to any that could possibly be detrimental to his future habits, moral, religious, or intellectual." *London Review*, No. II. p. 412, 413.

[t] Query. Do they always teach their children *other* prayers also, suitable to their present age? or do they account them altogether unfit for any communion with God, *as children?* This surely is supplying them with a provision of " strong meat," which they may hereafter " be able to bear," while they withhold the necessary immediate nourishment of milk.

serious evils, for the sake of a benefit immeasurably minute. To learn the same prayers, &c. in Latin or in Greek, would be, as an exercise of the memory, equally good, and in other respects, much better. For when the learner was afterwards, at a riper age, presented with a translation of these words, the sense would strike him, and would perhaps arouse his attention, and excite his devotional feelings. Every one who knows what it is to (not merely say his prayers, but) really pray, must be conscious that a continual effort is requisite to prevent a form of words with which he is very familiar, from sliding over the ear or the tongue, without being properly attended to, and accompanied by the heart and the understanding. Now the liability to this formal repetition of words, and the difficulty of avoiding it, must be greatly increased, if the words have been familiarly learnt by rote at a time when the understanding could not possibly accompany the recitation, from their being beyond a child's comprehension. Add to which, that a painful association is thus formed in the child's mind, between all the collects and texts, &c. he has been thus learning, and the idea of a dull, irksome, uninteresting, and unmeaning task.

Some however find that their children *do not* regard such repetitions as a painful, or even an uninteresting, task, but consider themselves, though they do not understand what they utter, as performing an act of devotion. Now this is precisely the case I have more particularly in view at present. The other just mentioned, of learning the words merely as an exercise of memory, is likely to *lead* to superstition; but *this* is itself superstitious. For what do the Romanists more, than make devotion consist in repeating a hallowed form of words, with a general intention indeed of praying, but without accompanying with the understanding the words uttered?

But, it may be replied, a child does understand *something* of what he is saying, if he does but understand that it is a prayer for some divine blessing; (an argument which may be, and is, urged by the Romanists in behalf of their Latin prayers;) while, on the other hand, the wisest man cannot be said *completely* to understand his prayers, since the nature of the Being he addresses must be mysterious to him. In many cases it happens that it is difficult to draw a precise line in theory, while, in practice, common sense leads every one to distinguish sufficiently. It is difficult, for instance, [vid. Hor. Epist. i. b. ii. line 35.] to lay down exactly how many years ago an author must have lived to be called " ancient ;"—how many grains of corn will make a heap, &c. &c. But as in other cases, so in this, men are seldom at a loss to perceive, with a sufficient approximation to truth for practical purposes, the distinction between what is, and what is not, " understood." Whenever a child is capable (which is generally at a very early age) of comprehending what prayer is, there must be *some* mode of expressing a prayer which will be intelligible to him; let *this* expression be then adopted; let him employ the form which he can *best* understand, and which may be subsequently modified and enlarged, as his understanding advances.

No doubt, a prayer thus adapted to the capacity of a child must be *childish;* how can any, *natural,* fervent, hearty devotions of a *child,* be otherwise than childish? Is it any disparagement to the devotions of grown men, that they are *human*, and not angelic? Let those who, for the sake of a form of words intrinsically better, teach children prayers not adapted to the puerile understanding—let them, I say, reflect on what grounds they can convict the Romanists of superstition on account of their Pater-nosters. If there be any intrinsic holiness in words which renders them in themselves acceptable, whether we worship "in Spirit and in Truth," or not, then, surely, Latin words may have this efficacy. But the intrinsic sanctity of the words of the Lord's prayer, for instance, is the same only as that of the wood of the True Cross. This was an instrument of the salvation of mankind when the Redeemer was offered upon it; the other is a means of grace when devoutly offered up "with the heart and with the understanding also" in the name of that Redeemer: but the child who repeats the words by rote is no more benefited by them, than by carrying about him a piece of the wood of the cross. And in both cases, positive harm is done instead of benefit, by the misdirection of religious feeling.

I have heard it urged, that a child would be

accounted a fool, if when sent to school he should be found unable to repeat the Lord's prayer. And certainly a child of average intelligence would usually be able, before the age supposed, to comprehend an *explanation* of that prayer; which of course should not be withheld one moment after it can be understood. But at all events, it is surely better, when that is the alternative, that a child should be reckoned a fool, without being so, than that he should *be* so, without its being detected; nor can it be doubted that there is real folly, whether apparent or not, in superstitiously attributing efficacy to an unmeaning form of words.

It is hardly necessary to observe, that the whole of the above reasoning applies equally to the practice of taking little children to church[u].

---

[u] Our Liturgy however is evidently neither adapted nor designed for children; even those of such an age as to be fully capable of joining in congregational worship, were there a service suitably composed on purpose for them. To frame and introduce such a service, would not, I think, be regarded as a trifling improvement, if we could but throughly get rid of the *principle* of the Romish lip-service. We cannot too much " take thought for the morrow," in matters relating to

V. There is also a strong tendency to superstition in all that relates to the place and mode of interment of a corpse. Many of my readers must have observed, that in a great number of church-yards, the north side is almost entirely untenanted by graves, through a certain vague notion of its being " unlucky" to be buried there. The origin I believe of this feeling is to be found in the Romish practice of praying for the dead. The principal entrance to almost all churches being on the south, one who was interred on the north, would be the less likely to obtain the passing prayers of his surviving neighbours, as they were proceeding to public worship. But however this may be, and however little the

---

" the kingdom of God and his righteousness ;" now children are emphatically the Morrow of Society; and in all that relates to religious and moral training, they are far the more important part of it; for we know that if we "train up a child in the way that he should go, when he is old he will not depart from it:" while, on the other hand, it is too often a vain attempt to remedy, by instruction to adults, the want of this early training. If we would but duly take care of children, grown people would generally take care of themselves.

origin of any superstition may be known or remembered, every thing, it is plain, *is* superstitious, and of the most mischievous class, which goes to connect the repose of the soul with any thing that takes place after a man's death. And continual watchfulness is requisite to prevent superstitions of this kind from being engrafted on the practice of interring the dead in church-yards, and performing the funeral-service over them. Nothing can be more proper than to choose such an occasion for the performance of devotional duties;—and to set aside a spot of ground for the decent interment of the dead;—nothing more natural and blameless, than the wish that our mortal remains should repose by the side of our friends and relatives: but the best things are liable to abuse; and the more sedulously, in most places, the Pastor studies the habitual sentiments of his flock, the less will he be disposed to regard as superfluous an especial watchfulness on this particular point;—a constant care to check the superstitious idea, that either the consecrated ground, (whether within or without the church,) or the funeral-service, have any thing to do with the individual's future destiny. And the more care and diligence is requisite for the *detection* of these and similar superstitions, inasmuch as those enslaved to them are often *ashamed* of them, and consequently disposed to conceal their real sentiments; especially from any one whom they perceive to be not disposed to sympathize with them. The exercise of this vigilance, accordingly, by any one who had not heretofore deemed it needful, would be very likely to bring to his knowledge much that would surprise him. I have known, for instance, a person, in speaking of a deceased neighbour, whose character had been irreligious and profligate, remark, how great a comfort it was to hear the words of the funeral-service read over her, " because, poor woman, she had been such a bad liver." I have heard of an instance again, of a superstition, probably before unsuspected, being accidentally brought to light, by the minister's having forbidden a particular corpse to be brought into the church, because the person had never frequented it when alive: the consequence of which was, that many old people began immediately to frequent the church, who had before been in the habit of absenting themselves.

§. 10. All these and numberless other such superstitions, it was the business of the Romish priesthood, not to introduce indeed, but to encourage and maintain, inasmuch as they almost all tend to increase the influence and wealth of the Hierarchy: let it be the Protestant-Pastor's business, not only to abstain from conniving at or favouring any thing of the kind, but (remembering that the original source of superstition is not in the Church of Rome, but in the heart of Man) to be ever on the watch against its inroads from various quarters, and in various shapes.

It is evidently not enough to avoid and discountenance every thing that is *in itself* superstitious;—such as (in addition to several of the things just mentioned) the consulting of pretended witches and soothsayers—faith in dreams and omens, and in lucky and unlucky days; with many superstitions of the same character; from which many even of the higher orders, in point of birth and station, are by no means wholly exempt, but which prevail to a much greater extent than I believe most persons who have not been much and confidentially conversant with the lower, and those somewhat above the lower, ranks, are at all inclined to suspect. Nor again, is it enough to reject and to discourage all such practices as, without being necessarily and in themselves superstitious, are, either generally, or at any particular time and place, peculiarly liable to be abused to a superstitious purpose, while they may, without any great loss, be dispensed with; such as were many of those practices of the Romish Church which our Reformers " brake in pieces," as Hezekiah did the brazen serpent; not as originally evil, but as the occasion of Superstition. All this, I say, is insufficient; because there are so many things which we *cannot* dispense with, which yet are continually liable to become no better than superstitious, through the superstitious character of " the natural man." We cannot dispense with the Sacraments which Christ appointed;—with prayer, both public and private;—with the reading of the Scriptures;—with instructions from the ministers of the Gospel;—with buildings and days set apart, either wholly or partly, for these purposes. Yet these, and every thing else of this kind, are perpetually liable to be abused, and indeed I fear perpetually *are* abused, into occasions of Superstition. Our prayers and our study of Scripture are, as I have above remarked, superstitious, when we trust in the efficacy of the words, without earnestly praying with the heart, and labouring to gain instruction in religion: the hearing of sermons is very commonly made an occasion of superstition, when a merit is attached to the act of hearing instruction, without labouring to understand, and profitably apply, that instruction. The sanctity belonging to the " Church" of Christ, i. e. to the body of believers who are " the Temple of the Holy Ghost which dwelleth in them[x]," is

[x] It is strange, and it is unfortunate, that so many should have not only overlooked the application of the term " Temple," by the Apostles, invariably to Christians *collectively*, never to the *individual* Christian, but should have even asserted the contrary, on the strength of one text, (1 Cor. vi. 19.) which according to all fair rules of interpretation exhibits (especially in the original Greek) the same sense as the rest

commonly transferred to the building in which a congregation assembles; while the veneration for that building is shewn not so much in an earnest endeavour that the prayers offered up, and the instructions given there, may be profitable to the soul, as in a superstitious feeling of satisfaction on the supposed merit of having, in bodily presence, frequented it during life, with perhaps a hope of future security, from the lifeless body's reposing within its walls. The Sacraments again, as I have said, become superstitious to those who deeply venerate, and trust in, the " outward visible sign," without thinking of any inward spiritual efforts after the inward spiritual grace. And yet, all these, and many other such occasions of Superstition, (for such they doubtless are often made,) are what we cannot dispense with. The more vigilance therefore must we use in our own case, and inculcate

of the passages where the word occurs. The Apostle must have had *some* meaning in his constant adherence to a form of speech by no means obvious; and that meaning, whatever it is, we are not likely to take in, if we do not attend to his language. See Hinds's *" Three Temples of the One God."*

upon others, in guarding against the inroads of Superstition.

In no point we may be assured is our spiritual Enemy more vigilant: he is ever ready, not merely to tempt us with the unmixed poison of known sin, but to corrupt even our food, and to taint even our medicine, with the venom of his falsehood. For Religion is the medicine of the soul; it is the designed and appropriate preventive and remedy for the evils of our nature; the subtle Tempter well knows that no other allurements to sin would be of so much avail, if this medicine were assiduously applied, and applied in unadulterated purity: and he knows that Superstition is the specific poison which may be the most easily blended with true Religion, and which will the most completely destroy its efficacy.

It is for us then to take heed that the " light which is in us be not darkness"—that our Religion be kept pure from the noxious admixture of Superstition: and it is for us to observe the errors of others, with a view to our own correction and to our own preservation; instead of contemplating " the mote that is in our brother's eye, while we behold not the beam that is in our own eye." Our conscience, if we carefully regulate, and diligently consult it, will be ready, after we have seen and condemned (which is no hard task) the faults of our neighbour, to furnish us (where there is need) with that salutary admonition, which the self-blinded King of Israel received from the mouth of the Prophet; "Thou art the man."

CHAPTER II.

VICARIOUS RELIGION.

§. 1. THE Apostle Paul, in many passages in his Epistles, characterises the Christian religion[a] as containing "Mysteries," that is, truths not discoverable by human reason, but made known by Divine revelation: as, for instance, in his first Epistle to Timothy[b], "without controversy great is the mystery of godliness."

And it is very important to observe, that in all the passages (and they are very numerous) in which he applies the word Mystery ($\mu\nu\sigma\tau\eta\rho\iota o\nu$) to the Christian faith, or to any part of it, the circumstance to which he is directing the reader's attention is, not the *concealment*, but the disclosure, of the mystery. He implies indeed that

---

[a] For that is evidently the meaning of the expression, ἡ εὐσεβεία, which our translators have rendered "Godliness."

[b] Chap. iii. 16.

the truths so described were *formerly* unknown, and could not be known by man's unaided powers; but he speaks of them as now at length laid open, by the gracious dispensation of Providence; as no longer concealed, except from those who wilfully shut their eyes against the light of divine revelation: " if our Gospel is hid, it is hid to them that are lost, whom the god of this world hath blinded:" and his own office in " proclaiming the good tidings c" of this revelation, he describes as " making known the mystery of the Gospel," "which was kept secret since the world began, but now is made *manifest.*"

Not that the Apostle meant to imply but that after all, the nature and designs of the Most High must be by us very imperfectly understood; but the circumstance to which he is especially calling attention is, not the unrevealed, but the revealed—not the unintelligible, but the explained—portion of the divine dispensations.

^c This we should always remember is the strict sense of the phrase κηρύσσειν τὸ Εὐαγγέλιον, which we usually render, in words which by familiarity have almost lost their original force, " preaching the Gospel."

And this he does, in manifest allusion to the mysteries of the ancient pagan religions; with which, in this respect, he contrasts Christianity; inasmuch as in this last there was not, as among the Pagans, a distinction between the initiated and the uninitiated;—a revelation to some of the worshippers, of certain holy secrets, from which the rest were excluded; nor *great* mysteries and *lesser* mysteries, (as the Eleusinian,) in which different persons were initiated; but, on the contrary, the " *great*" mysteries of the Christian faith (μέγα μυστήριον) were made known, as far as it is expedient and possible for man to know them, to all alike, whether Jew or Gentile, who were but willing to embrace the truth: and " to know the fellowship" (i. e. the common participation) " of the mystery," κοινωνία τοῦ μυστήριου, was offered to all. There was not one system of religion for a certain favoured few, and another, for the mass of believers; but the great " mystery of godliness" was made accessible, gradually indeed, in proportion as they were able to bear it, but universally. To all Christ's disciples it was " given to know the mysteries of the kingdom of heaven [d];" there was " one Lord, one faith, one baptism," and (though with diversity of gifts) one and the same Spirit, sanctifying the Church, and dwelling in all its members.

The opposite system to this—that of recognizing different degrees of access to the Deity, and of keeping certain sacred rites and holy secrets confined to a few, and set apart from the multitude—is one of the most remarkable characteristics of natural religion; by which expression I mean, not what is commonly, though improperly, so called; but, such a religious system as men *naturally* fall into, when left to themselves.

---

[d] Matt. xiii. 11. " To you it is given to know the mysteries of the kingdom," &c. An objection has been raised from this passage, because it is said that the others, viz. those who were not disciples, were not admitted to the same advantage. But why did they not *become* disciples? If Jesus had rested his claims on the apparent reasonableness of what He taught, it would have been most unfair to require men to join Him before they fully understood it: but his claim rested on the " mighty works," which afforded sufficient proof of his coming from God.

The case of the Eleusinian mysteries, above alluded to, is only one instance out of many. Indeed I believe there is hardly any system of Paganism with which we are acquainted, that has not some articles of faith—some religious rites—some kind of pretended theological knowledge—confined, either to the priests, or to some privileged Order of men, and from which the great body of worshippers is either excluded, or at least exempted.

It might be expected therefore that this character should be found (as in fact it is) in the Romish system; which I have already described as the gradual and (if I may be allowed the expression) spontaneous corruption of Christianity, by the natural unrestrained workings of the human mind.

Men readily perceived, what indeed is very true, that those who have leisure and abilities beyond what falls to the lot of the generality, are enabled, and may be expected, to acquire a larger share of learning, generally, and, among the rest, of theological learning: while the proper *object* of this theological learning (under such a system as that of Christianity) is often lost sight of; viz. to establish the authority, and ascertain and *explain* the meaning, of the sacred writings. And again, men readily perceived, that there are many points connected with religion which are in a great degree beyond their comprehension; without accurately distinguishing *which* are so, from their own deficiency in learning, and which, from being beyond the reach of the human faculties.

The learned, on the other hand, or such as aspired to that character, felt, of course, the natural love of *distinction* the more gratified, in proportion as their studies were supposed to be directed to points the most abstruse and recondite—to some knowledge respecting things divine, beyond the understanding, and too sacred for the inquiries, of ordinary men.

At the same time, the natural inquisitiveness of the human mind after speculative knowledge, especially on the most exalted subjects, having led theologians to overlook the *practical* character of the Christian revelation, and to indulge in presumptuous disquisitions as to the *intrinsic* nature of the Deity, this circumstance could not but contribute still more to set apart a certain portion of (supposed) divine knowledge as unnecessary, and unfit, for vulgar contemplation. Mysterious doctrines unconnected with Christian practice, at least with such practice as was required from the great mass of Christians, it was sufficient that they should assent to with implicit faith, without attempting to examine the proofs of such matters—to understand the doctrines themselves—or even to know what they were: " I do not presume, nor am able, to comprehend the Mysteries of the Faith, but leave them to my spiritual guides;—I believe all that the Holy Catholic Church receives;"—such was the language—such the easy and compendious confession of faith—which resulted from the indolence—the spiritual carelessness—the weakness, and the dishonest ambition, of human nature.

The unprofitable, absurd, presumptuous, and profane speculations of scholastic theologians (not all of them members of the Romish Church) which are extant, afford a melancholy specimen of the fruits of this mistake as to the Christian Mysteries—this " corruption from the *simplicity* that is in Christ."

Specimens of this " philosophy and vain deceit"—such as are to be found in various dissertations on what are called the mysterious doctrines of the Christian faith—such as I cannot bring myself to transcribe, and cannot even think of without shuddering—it may be sometimes a profitable though a painful task to peruse, in order to estimate duly, as a warning and admonition to ourselves, the effects of misapplied learning and misdirected ingenuity. To select one instance out of many, no point in these systems of speculative theology has so much exercised the perverted powers of divines of this stamp, as the mystery of the Trinity[e]; or as *they* might with more propriety have called it, the mystery of the divine *Unity:* for though in itself the doctrine so sedulously inculcated throughout the Scriptures that there is but One God, seems to present no revolting difficulty, yet, on rising from the disquisitions of many scholastic divines

---

[e] The selection of this particular doctrine by way of illustration was suggested by the circumstance, that the Discourse, of which the following pages contain the substance, was delivered before the University on Trinity-Sunday. I have retained the passage, because I can think of no other instance that better illustrates what has been said.

on the inherent distinctions of the three Divine Persons, a candid reader cannot but feel that *they* have made the Unity of God the great and difficult mystery[f]; and have in fact so nearly

---

[f] It is however important to remark, that though the Unity of the Deity is not *in itself* a doctrine of very mysterious difficulty, it is one which is the more earnestly dwelt on in Scripture, besides other reasons, for one resulting from the tone of the Scriptures themselves. For they would, *but for* these express declarations, naturally lead the reader either to believe in three Gods, or at least to be in doubt on the question. The doctrine of the Trinity is not so much *declared* as a distinct article of faith, as it is *implied* by the whole history recorded, and views every where taken, in Scripture, of God's threefold manifestation of Himself; which are such as would present to our minds nothing inconsistent with the agency of three Divine Beings acting in concert, were it not that such sedulous care is taken to assure us of the numerical Unity of the God thus manifested to us;—that in the Son " dwelleth all the fulness of the Godhead," &c. &c. See Essay vii. (Second Series,) p. 234, 235. and Essay ix. p. 277—281. See also Hinds's " Three Temples of the One God," p. 129, 132. for a most luminous view of this important subject.

The reader is also referred to the Articles " One," and " Person," in the Appendix to the " Elements of Logic." It has been doubted whether there is any foundation for the suspicion I have there expressed, that the language of some

explained it away, and so bewildered the minds of their disciples, as to drive them to withdraw

divines has a leaning towards Tritheism. The following extract will at once explain my meaning, and prove, I conceive, satisfactorily, that my apprehensions are not altogether groundless. It is taken from a work of considerable merit, and which has obtained not only much popularity, but also a peculiarly high description of patronage. Several of my readers will perhaps recognize the passage; but I purposely avoid naming the book, because it is not my object to discuss the merits of this or that individual work, but to call attention to the notions which are afloat in the world, generally; and I am so far from designing to particularize the work in question, as containing any thing novel, peculiar, likely to be generally offensive, and at variance with prevailing opinions, that my meaning is the very reverse.

" When the great Creator had finished the rest of his works, wanting another creature to rule them all, and as their Priest, to adore him in their name, he said, ' Let us make man in our own image, after our likeness.' In the creation of other things all is done with the tone of command, or with a mere volition. ' Let there be light; let there be a firmament'; let the earth bring forth so and so.' But when man is to be made—a creature who is to be endued with reason and intelligence—the very image of the Maker—he uses an expression which indicates deliberation and counsel; he consults with some other august Beings, (the two remaining Per-

their thoughts habitually and deliberately from every thing connected with the subject⁵; as the only mode left for the unlearned to keep clear of error. Yet it might have occurred, one would have thought, to both parties, that learning cannot advance one man beyond another in the comprehension of things which are confessedly beyond the reach of the human faculties altogether;—that in total darkness, or in respect of objects beyond our horizon, the clearest and the dimmest sight are on a level;—and that of

sons of the Trinity, no doubt,) of whom, as well as of himself, man was to be both the workmanship and the resemblance."

If this passage had stood alone in the Jewish Scriptures, or if the Jews had interpreted it, as this writer has done, without any reference to the other passages of Scripture which serve to qualify and guard it, they would doubtless (as the above extract seems to shew) have adopted nearly the same hypothesis as was long afterward broached by Arius;—that the supreme God acts in concert " with some other august Beings!"

⁵ I am enabled to state this as no mere conjecture or suspicion, but as a matter of *fact* coming within my own experience; I mean, in respect of sundry individual cases; and it is individual cases only that come within the province of experience.

matters relating to the Deity and revealed by Him, not as a special secret, to a favoured few, but to all who would hear his voice, and which cannot be discovered any otherwise than through this revelation—of these, none *need* know less, and none *can* know more, than the Almighty has thus revealed.

The nature of God as He *is in Himself*, can never be comprehended by the wisest of us his creatures; but the doctrine of the Trinity, and the rest of the mysteries of the Gospel, as far as they *relate to us*, since He *has* thought fit to reveal these to us in the Gospel, every Christian is allowed, and is bound, to learn from that Revelation " of the mystery which was secret from the beginning of the world, but now is *made manifest*[h]." And the doctrine of the Trinity, (which is perhaps the oftenest of any treated as a speculative truth about which none but learned divines need trouble themselves,) as it is a summary of that faith into[i] which we are baptized, and the

---

[h] Rom. xvi. 25.

[i] " Teach all nations, baptizing them *into* the name (εἰς τὸ ὄνομα) of the Father, and of the Son, and of the Holy Ghost:" this is evidently the right rendering of the original words,

key-stone of the Christian system, ought to be set forth continually and universally, as the support of every part of the building of the Christian faith, and the Christian life: reference should be made to it, not merely on some stated solemn occasions, as to an abstruse tenet to be assented to, and then laid aside, but perpetually, as to a practical doctrine, connected with every other point of religious belief and conduct.

§. 2. In no point perhaps has the real origin of the Romish corruptions been more imperfectly perceived, than in the one now before us—the setting apart of certain religious dogmas—duties—privileges—in short, certain portions of Christianity, as confined to a distinct class of men, and in which the laity were either not allowed or not required to have a share. We are accustomed

and conveys the sense which must have been meant, viz. that the baptized convert was enrolled and enlisted, as it were, into the service of the Father, the Son, and the Holy Ghost. The Vulgate Latin has "*in* nomine," and our translation, (perhaps from too great reverence for that authority,) "*in* the name;" which does violence to the original, and introduces a different idea, quite inappropriate.

to hear much of priestcraft—of the subtle arts of designing men, who imposed on the simplicity of an ignorant people, and persuaded them to believe that they, the priests, alone understood the nature of the Deity—the proper mode in which to propitiate Him—and the mysterious doctrines to which the others were to give their implicit assent; and the poor deluded people are represented as prevailed on against their better judgment, by the sophistry, and promises, and threats, of these crafty impostors, to make *them* the keepers of their consciences—their mediators, and substitutes in the service of God, and their despotic spiritual rulers.

There is undoubtedly much truth in such a representation; but it leaves on the mind an erroneous impression, because it is (at the utmost) only *half* the truth.

If indeed in any country, priests had been Beings of a different species—or a distinct Caste, as in some of the Pagan nations where the priesthood is hereditary;—if this race had been distinguished from the people by intellectual superiority and moral depravity, and if the people had been sincerely desirous of knowing, and serving, and obeying God for themselves, but had been persuaded by these demons in human form that this was impossible, and that the laity must trust *them* to perform what was requisite, in their stead, and submit implicitly to their guidance—then indeed there would be ground for regarding priestcraft as altogether the work of the priests, and in no degree, of the people. But we should remember, that in every age and country, (even where they were, as the Romish priests were not, a distinct Caste,) priests must have been mere men, of like passions with their brethren; and though sometimes they might have, on the whole, a considerable intellectual superiority, yet it must always have been impossible to delude men into the reception of such gross absurdities, if they had not found in them a readiness—nay, a craving—for delusion. The reply which is recorded of a Romish priest, is, (not in the sight of God indeed, but) as far as regards any complaint on the part of the laity, a satisfactory defence; when taxed with some of the monstrous impostures of his Church, his answer was, " Populus vult decipi, et decipiatur." Such indeed was the case of Aaron, and similar the defence he offered, for making the Israelites an image, at their desire. Let it not be forgotten, that the *first recorded* instance of departure from purity of worship, as established by the revelation to the Israelites, was forced on the *priest* by the *people*.

The truth is, mankind have an innate propensity, as to other errors, so, to that of endeavouring to serve God by proxy;—to commit to some distinct order of men the care of their religious concerns, in the same manner as they confide the care of their bodily health to the physician, and of their legal transactions to the lawyer; deeming it sufficient to follow implicitly their directions, without attempting themselves to become acquainted with the *mysteries* of medicine or of law [k]. Even thus are

---

[k] Nothing is more mischievous than an incorrect analogy that is constantly before us, and familiar to our minds. Like a distorted mirror in the apartment we inhabit, it produces, not an insulated or occasional error, but a deep-seated and habitual false impression. Now nothing can be more familiar than the seeming analogy between the several professions. Men may rather be said habitually to feel, than distinctly to maintain, (indeed the falsehood would be easily detected in a formal assertion,) that as the soldier is in respect of military,

they willing and desirous that others should study, and should understand, the mysterious doctrines of religion in their stead—should practise, in their stead, some more exalted kind of piety and of virtue—and should offer prayers and sacrifices on their behalf, both in their lifetime and after their death. For man, except when unusually depraved, retains enough of the image of his Maker, to have a natural reverence for religion, and a desire that God should be worshipped; but, through the corruption of his nature, his heart is (except when divinely purified) too much alienated from God to take delight in serving Him. Hence, the disposition men have ever shewn, to substitute the devotion of the Priest for their own;—to leave the duties of piety in his hands—and to let him serve God *in their stead.* This disposition is not so much the *consequence,* as itself the origin, of priestcraft. The Romish hierarchy did but take advantage from time to time of this natural propensity, by engrafting successively on its system

and the sailor, in respect of naval affairs, and the physician, in respect of remedies for bodily disease, and the lawyer, in legal matters, so is the clergyman in respect of religion.

such practices and points of doctrine as favoured it, and which were naturally converted into a source of profit and influence to the priesthood. Hence the gradual transformation of the Christian minister—the Presbyter—into the sacrificing priest, the Hiereus, (in Latin, " Sacerdos ;" as the Romanists call theirs,) of the Jewish and Pagan religions. This last is an error of which no inconsiderable remains are to be traced in the minds of Protestants, and on which, as it appears to me to be very important, I shall beg to be indulged in making some more particular observations.

§. 3. [1] That the English word PRIEST is frequently employed for the rendering of two different words in Greek, *viz.* Ἱερεὺς, and Πρεσβύτερος, (from the latter of which our " Presbyter" or " Priest" is derived,) is a circumstance of which no scholar can be ignorant indeed, but which is not in

---

[1] The passage which follows I have taken the liberty of extracting, in substance, and nearly in words, from a Discourse delivered before the University of Oxford, on the 5th of Nov. 1821, and published with the second edition of the Bampton Lectures.

general sufficiently attended to: for it is not the same thing to be merely *acquainted* with the ambiguity of a word, and to be practically aware of it, and watchful of the consequences connected with it. And it is, I conceive, of no small importance that this ambiguity should be carefully and frequently explained to those who are ignorant of the original language of the Old Testament.

Our own name for the Ministers of our own religion, we naturally apply to the *Ministers* (in whatever sense) of any other religion; but the two words which have thus come to be translated " Priest," seem by no means to be used synonymously. The Priests, both of the Jews and of Pagan nations[m], constantly bear, in the sacred writers, the title of *Hiereus;* which title they never apply to any of the Christian Ministers ordained by the Apostles. These are called by the title of *Episcopos*, (literally Superintendant; whence our English word " Bishop;") *Presbyteros*, literally Elder, and so rendered by our translators, probably to avoid the ambiguity just alluded to; though the very word " Presbyter" or " Priest," is but a corruption of that name:

[m] Acts xiv. 13.

and—*Diaconos*, literally "Minister;" from which our word Deacon is but slightly altered.

These titles, from their original vague and general signification, became gradually not only restricted in great measure to Christian Ministers, but also more precisely distinguished from each other than at first they had been; so as to be appropriated respectively to the different orders of those Ministers, instead of being applied indiscriminately. But no mention is made, by the sacred writers, of any such office being established by the Apostles, as that of "Priest" in the other sense, *viz. Hiereus;*—Priest, in short, such as we find mentioned, under that name, in Scripture.

Now this alone would surely be a strong presumption that they regarded the two offices as essentially distinct; for they must have been perfectly familiar with the *name*; and had they intended to institute the same *office*, or one very similar to it, we cannot but suppose they would have employed that name[n]. The mere circum-

---

[n] For it should never be forgotten, that Christianity is the offspring of Judaism, and that all the institutions and regulations of the Christian Church emanated from men who had

stance that the Christian religion is very *different* from all others, would, of itself, have been no reason against this; for the difference is infinite between the divinely-instituted religion of the Jews, and the idolatrous superstitions of the heathen; and yet, from similarity of office, the word *Hiereus* is applied by the sacred writers to the Ministers of both religions.

The difference of names, then, is, in such a case as this, a matter of no trifling importance, but would, even of itself, lead us to infer a difference of *things*, and to conclude that the Apostles regarded their religion as having no Priest at all, (in the sense of Ἱερεὺς,) except Christ Jesus, of whom indeed all the Levitical Priests were but types.

§. 4. It should next be considered what was the nature of that office which was exercised by the Jewish and by the Pagan Priests; and which, according to the Apostle, belonged, after the establishment of Christ's kingdom, to Him alone.

been brought up as Jews, and who would not have deviated from what they had been used to, on slight grounds

The Priests of the Israelites were appointed by the Almighty himself, for the express purpose of offering *sacrifices*, in the name and on the behalf of the people; they alone were allowed to make oblations and burn incense before the Lord: it was through them that the people were to approach Him, that their service might be acceptable: a very great portion of the Jewish religion consisted in the performance of certain ceremonial rites, most of which could only be duly performed by the Priests, or through their mediation and assistance; they were to make *intercession* and *atonement* for offenders; they, in short, were the *mediators* between God and man.

It is true the Israelites were a sacred *nation*, and are called in Scripture a "kingdom of Priests;" but it is plain that this is not to be understood as admitting them all indiscriminately to the exercise of the sacred offices just mentioned; since the most tremendous punishments were denounced (of whose infliction examples are recorded) against any who, not being of the seed of Aaron, presumed to take upon them to burn incense and make oblations.

But it was requisite to impress on the minds

of the Israelites that they were not to entertain the notion (which appears to have been not uncommon among the heathen) that religion was the exclusive concern of the Priests: they, on the contrary, were required to worship God themselves—to conform to his ordinances—to keep themselves pure from all defilement, moral or ceremonial—and to practise all their duties out of reverence to God, their Lawgiver and King; they were, in short, to be Priests in piety of heart and holiness of life. And in the same sense Peter calls Christians " a royal Priesthood;" and John, in the Apocalypse, speaks of them as " Kings and Priests;" evidently meaning that they were dedicated to Christ, and were bound to offer up themselves as a living sacrifice devoted to Him. For it is most important to observe, that when the title of Priest is applied *to Christians*, it is applied to *all* of them.

There may have been another intention also in calling the Israelites a kingdom of Priests; *viz.* to point out that the mysteries of their religion (which among the Pagans were in general kept secret among the Priests, or some select number whom these admitted to the knowledge of them) were revealed, as far as they were revealed at all, to the whole of this favoured nation. Many parts indeed of the Mosaic institutions were but imperfectly understood by any, as to their object and signification; but nothing seems to have been imparted to the Priests which was withheld from the people. This very striking distinction is remarked by Josephus, who observes, that such religious mysteries as, among the heathen, were concealed by the Priests, were imparted to the whole Jewish nation.

That there was, however, a distinct order of Priests, properly so called, set apart for a peculiar purpose, is undeniable and undisputed.

Among the Pagans, whose institutions appear to have been, in great measure, corrupt imitations of those of the patriarchal religion, we find, as before, Priests, who were principally, if not exclusively, the offerers of sacrifices, in behalf of the State and of individuals—intercessors—supplicating and making atonement for others—mediators between Man and the object of his worship.

This peculiarity of office was even carried to the length of an abuse: (I speak now of the abuses introduced into the *institutions* of the Pagans, in contradistinction to the absurdities of their *faith*:) there seems to have been (as has been already hinted) a strong tendency to regard all religion as exclusively the concern of the Priests;—that they were to be the sole depositaries of the mysteries of things sacred;—that a high degree of holiness of life and devotion were required of them alone;—that they were to be religious, as it were, instead of the people;—and that men had only to shew due respect to the Priests, and leave to them the service of the Deity; just as they commit the defence of the state to soldiers, and the cure of their diseases, to physicians. Against such notions (as was before remarked) the Israelites were studiously, and not without reason, cautioned.

The office of Priest, then, in that sense of the word which I am now considering, *viz.* as equivalent to *Hiereus*, being such as has been described, it follows that, in *our* religion, the *only* Priest, in that sense, is Jesus Christ himself; to whom consequently, and to whom alone, under the Gospel, the title is applied by the inspired writers. He alone has offered up an atoning *sacrifice* for us, even the sacrifice of his own blood; He " ever liveth to make *intercession* for us;" He is the " one *Mediator* between God and man ;" " through Him we have access to the Father ;" and " no man cometh unto the Father but by Him."

§. 5. As for the Ministers whom He, and his Apostles, and their successors, appointed, they are completely distinct from Priests in the former sense, in office, as well as in name. Of this office one principal part is, that it belongs to them (not exclusively indeed, but principally and especially) to preach the Gospel—to maintain order and decency in their religious assemblies, and Christian discipline, generally—to instruct, exhort, admonish, and spiritually govern, Christ's flock. His command was, to " go and teach all nations ;"—to " preach the Gospel to every creature :" and these Christian Ministers are called in the Epistle to the Hebrews, " those that bear rule over them, and watch for their souls, as they that must give an account." Now it is worthy of remark, that the office I am at present speaking of made no part of the especial duties of a Priest, in the other sense, such as those of the Jews, and of the Pagans. Among the former, it was not so much the family of Aaron. as the whole tribe of Levi, that seem to have been set aside for the purpose of *teaching* the Law: and even to these it was so far from being in any degree confined, that persons of any tribe might teach publicly in the synagogues on the Sabbath day; as was done by our Lord himself, who was of the tribe of Judah; and by Paul, of the tribe of Benjamin, without any objection being raised: whereas an intrusion into the Priest's office would have been vehemently resented.

And as for the Pagan Priests, *their* business was rather to conceal, than to explain, the mysteries of their religion;—to keep the people in darkness, than to enlighten them. Accordingly, the moral improvement of the people, among the ancients, seems to have been considered as the proper care of the legislator, whose laws and systems of public education generally had this object in view. To these, and to the public disputations of philosophers, but by no means to the Priests of their religion, they appear to have looked for instruction in their duty.

That the Christian Ministry, on the contrary,

were appointed, in great measure, if not principally, for the express purpose of giving religious instruction and admonition, is clearly proved both by the practice of the Apostles themselves, and by Paul's directions to Timothy and to Titus.

Another, and that a peculiar and exclusive office of the Christian Ministers, at least according to the practice of most Churches, is, the administration of the sacraments of Baptism and of the Lord's Supper. But this administration does not at all assimilate the Christian Priesthood to the Pagan or the Jewish. The former of these rites is, in the first place, an admission into the visible Church; and therefore very suitably received at the hands of those whose especial business is to *instruct* and examine those who are candidates for Baptism, as adults, or who have been baptized in their infancy; and in the second place, it is an admission to a participation in the gifts of the Spirit; without which the Church itself, and the formal admission into it, would be an empty mockery. The treasury, as it were, of divine grace is then thrown open, to which we may resort when a sufficient maturity of years enables us to understand our wants, and we are inclined to apply for their relief. It is not, let it be observed, through the mediation of an earthly Priest that we are admitted to offer our supplications before God's mercy-seat; we are authorized, by virtue of this sacred rite, to appear, as it were, in his presence, ourselves, needing no intercessor with the Father, but his Son Jesus Christ, both God and man. "Having therefore," says Paul, "*boldness* to enter into the holiest by the blood of Jesus, by a new and living way, which he hath consecrated for us, and having an High Priest over the house of God, let us draw near with a true heart, in full *assurance* of faith, having our hearts sprinkled from an evil conscience, and our bodies washed with pure water."

The sacrament of the Lord's Supper, again, is not, as the Romanists impiously pretend, a fresh sacrifice, but manifestly a celebration of the one already made; and the rite seems plainly to have been ordained for the express purpose (among others) of fixing our minds on the great and single oblation of himself, made by the only High Priest, once for all;—that great High Priest who has no earthly successor. And *all* the communicants are alike partakers, spiritually, of the body and blood of Christ, (i. e. of the Spirit of Christ, represented by his Flesh and Blood, as these again are, by the Bread and Wine°,) provided *they themselves* are in a sanctified and right frame of mind. It is on the personal holiness of the communicant, not of the Minister, that the efficacy of this Sacrament depends; *he*, so far from offering any sacrifice himself, refers them to the sacrifice already made by another.

Such being then the respective offices of these two orders of men, (both now commonly called in English "Priests," but originally distinguished by the names of Ἱερεὺς and Πρεσβύτερος,) we may assert, that the word in question is *ambiguous;* denoting, when thus applied to both, two things, essentially distinct. It is not merely a comprehensive term, embracing two species under one class, but rather an equivocal term, applied, in different senses, to two things of different classes. Thus the word Publican, for instance, is ambiguous when applied to a "tax-gatherer" and an "innkeeper;"

° See note on the Eucharist appended to Essay viii. Second Series.

though "Man," which is a still more comprehensive term, may be applied to both without ambiguity; because, however widely they differ, it denotes them only so far forth as they agree; in short, it is applied to them *in the same sense;* which "Publican" is not. No more is "Priest," when applied to the "Hiereus" and the "Presbyteros." At least it must be admitted, that what is most essential to each respectively, is wanting in the other. The essential characteristic of the Jewish Priests, was, (not their being *Ministers* of religion; for that, in a certain sense, all the Levites were; but) their offering *sacrifices*, and making atonement and intercession for the people: whereas of the Christian Minister the especial office is religious instruction, regulation of the religious assemblies, and of the religious and moral conduct, of the people, generally; (an office corresponding to that of the Jewish Elders or Presbyters, and of the "Rulers of Synagogues,") and the administration of rites totally different in their nature from the offering of sacrifices;—totally precluding the idea of *his* making himself the mediator between God and man.

§. 6. The confounding together, then, through the ambiguity of language, two things thus essentially distinct, may well be expected to mislead, not only such as are ignorant of the distinction, but all who do not carefully attend to it, and keep it steadily in view. If we are but careful not to lose sight of the two meanings of the word "Priest"—the broad distinction between Ἱερεὺς and Πρεσβύτερος—we shall run no risk of being either seduced or silenced by all the idle clamours that are afloat about priestcraft. Our readiest and shortest answer will be, that Christianity (I mean Christianity as found in Scripture, not as perverted by the Romish Church, which claims an authority independent of Scripture) has no priestcraft, for this simple reason, that it has (in that sense of the word in which our opponents employ it) *no Priest on earth.*

And it is worthy of remark how striking a *peculiarity* this is in our religion; there being probably no religion in the world, certainly none that has ever prevailed among the more celebrated nations, which has not Priests in the same sense in which the Levitical Priests and those of the ancient Greeks and Romans are so called. Now every peculiarity of our religion is worth noticing, with a view to the confirmation of our faith, even though it may not at first sight strike us as a distinguishing *excellence:* for that our religion should differ from all others, in points in which they all agree, is a presumption at least that it is not drawn from the same origin. And the presumption is the stronger, inasmuch as the difference I have been speaking of is not slight or verbal, but real and essential. The Priesthood of Pagan nations, and that of our own, are not merely *unlike*, but, in the most essential points, even *opposite*. *They* offer sacrifices for the people; *we* refer them to a sacrifice made by another; *they* profess to be the mediators through whom the Deity is to be addressed; *we* teach them to look to a heavenly Mediator, and in his name boldly to approach God's mercy-seat themselves: *they* study to conceal the mysteries of religion; *we* labour to make them known: *they* have, for the most part, hidden sacred books, which none but a chosen few may look into; *we* teach and exhort men to study the word of God themselves: *they* strive to keep the people in darkness, and to stifle inquiry; *we* make it our business to enlighten them; urging them to " search the Scriptures"—to " prove all things—and to hold fast that which is right:" *they* practise the duties of their religion *instead* of the people; *we* instruct and admonish all to practise them for themselves. And it may be added, that *they* in general teach, that a devoted confidence in them and obedience to their commands, will serve as a substitute for a moral life; while *we* declare to them from Scripture, that it is in vain to call Jesus Lord, if they " do not the things which He says."

Now if the Jews be justly condemned, who crucified our Lord between two thieves—thus studiously " numbering with the transgressors" of the vilest kind, the only man who never transgressed—it is awful to think what account those will have to render at the last day, who labour to vilify this religion, by confounding it with the grossest systems of human imposture and superstition, in those very points in which the two are not only different, but absolutely *contrasted*.

§. 7. Great occasion however (as I have said) has been afforded for the enemies of our faith to blaspheme, by the corruptions which the Romish Church has sanctioned, especially in what regards the Christian Priesthood. She has, in fact, in a great degree, transformed the Presbyter—the Priest of the Gospel dispensation—into the Hiereus, or Levitical Priest: thus derogating from the honour of the one great High Priest, and altering some of the most characteristic features of his religion, into something more like Judaism or Paganism than Christianity.

The Romish Priest professes, like the Jewish, to offer sacrifice (the sacrifice of the mass) to propitiate God towards himself and his congregation: the efficacy of that sacrifice is made to depend on sincerity and rectitude of intention, not in the *communicants* themselves, but in the *Priest;* he, assuming the character of a mediator and intercessor, prays, not *with*, but *for*, the people, in a tongue unknown to them, and in an inaudible voice: the whole style and character of the service being evidently far different from what the Apostle must have intended, in commanding us to " pray for one another." The

Romish Priest undertakes to reconcile transgressors with the Almighty, by prescribing penances, to be performed by them, in order to obtain *his* absolution; and, profanely copying our only High Priest, pretends to transfer to them his own merits, or those of the saints. He, like a Pagan, rather than a Jewish, Priest, keeps hidden from the people the volume of their faith, that they may with ignorant reverence submit to the dominion of error, instead of being " made free by the truth," which he was expressly commissioned to make known; thus hiding the " candle under a bushel," which was designed to " be a light to lighten the nations."

In short, whoever will minutely examine, with this view, the errors of the Romish Church, will find that a very large and important portion of them may be comprehended under this one general censure, that they have destroyed the true character of the Christian Priesthood; substituting for it, in great measure, what cannot be called a Priesthood, except in a different sense of the word. They have, in short, gone far towards changing the office of Presbyter into that of Hiereus. Against that Church, therefore, the charge of priestcraft may but too justly be brought.

A natural consequence of this error, indeed, properly speaking, a part of it, is that further approach to Judaism, the error of regarding a Christian place of worship as answering to the *Temple*—" the House of God" in Jerusalem; whereas it really corresponds to a Jewish *synagogue*. And thus the reverence due to the real Temple of the Lord now subsisting among us and within us (" ye are the Temple of the Holy Ghost which dwelleth in you") is transferred from the people— the " lively stones" of God's House, to the building in which they assemble [p]. On the same principle, the Table used for the celebration of the Eucharist is often called, (consistently, by Romanists, but inconsistently, by Protestants,) the " Altar."

Part of the same system again was the performance of divine service in an unknown tongue —the concealment of the sacred mysteries of the Christian faith behind the veil of a dead language—and the opposition made to the transla-

---

[p] See Hinds's Three Temples of the One God.

tion of the Scriptures into the vernacular languages.

§. 8. If any one doubts the existence, among Protestants of the present day, of a like principle, he may find but too convincing a proof of it in the opposition still made by some, to the education of the poor. Surely many of those who profess the greatest abhorrence of Romish errors, have never considered that this denial of the Scriptures to the people is one of the worst of them; and that whether the Bible is in Latin or in English, makes little difference to one who cannot read. Nor do such persons consider, that it was (if I may so speak) the great boast of the Founder of our Faith, that "to the poor the Gospel was preached:" so that if his religion be not really calculated for these, his pretensions must have been unfounded. The very truth of his divine mission is at issue on this question.

And yet if it were asked of any one, Romanist or Protestant, who professes to acknowledge the divine origin of the Christian religion, whether that religion was designed for the great mass of the people, or merely for a few of the higher classes, he would be sure to answer, that it was intended for all mankind. And in proof of this, he might cite numerous passages of the Scriptures which imply it; such as the command of our Lord to " preach the Gospel to every creature," and his application, just above noticed, of the prophecy, " to the poor the Gospel is preached." And he would represent it (and justly) as a point of the highest importance, as I have said, towards our belief in the Christian religion, that we should regard it as suited to all mankind—as one which all, above the condition of mere savages, are capable of embracing; because otherwise it cannot be a true revelation. For the first founders of it plainly had this design; Jesus Christ himself did certainly intend his religion for high and low, rich and poor; and therefore if it be not one which the lower ranks of society are *capable* of embracing, He, the founder of it, must have been mistaken in his calculation—must have been ignorant either of the character of his own religion, or of the nature of man; which would of course imply that He could not have been divinely inspired. The systems of Aristotle or Plato, of Newton or Locke, may, conceivably, be very true, although the mass of mankind cannot comprehend them, because they were never intended for the mass of mankind: but the Christian religion was; and therefore it cannot really be a divine revelation, unless it be such as men in general can understand and embrace.

And yet, though such would be the answer which almost all believers would give, in words, if such a question were put, there are, as I have said, not a few who, in *practice*, give a contrary answer. I mean, that they act as if the Christian religion were *not* designed for the lower orders, but only for a small portion of mankind. For this those do, who, under the pretence that the labouring classes " need not be profound theologians," consider it unnecessary, or even mischievous, to give them such an education as may enable them to study for themselves the Scriptures, and the explanations needful for the understanding of them. And yet they profess to hold, that the Christian religion *was* meant to be embraced by people of all ranks.

Whence comes this contradiction? this inconsistency of their practical views with their professed belief? It arises, I conceive, from their not considering what the Christian religion is, and what is meant by embracing it. When they say that they believe it to be designed for the mass of the people, and yet that these need not, or should not, be educated, what they mean is this: that it is possible for a man without any education, to be sober, honest, industrious, contented, &c., and that sobriety, honesty, and the rest, are Christian virtues; and that, consequently, a man may be a good practical Christian without any education. What they mean, in short, by a man's being a good Christian, is his doing those things which are enjoined to Christians, and abstaining from those things which are forbidden. To know on what grounds the Christian religion is to be believed, to understand any thing of its doctrines—to adopt or to comprehend any Christian motives and principles of conduct—all this they conceive to be unnecessary, except for the clergy and the higher classes, as long as a man's conduct is but right. Now this is in fact, as I have said, the Romish system; which is so natural to man, that under one shape or another, it is continually springing up under new names. The Romish Church, we know, used to forbid, and, as long as it was possible, prevented, the Scriptures being translated into the popular languages; and enjoined the people not to attempt to pry into religious questions for themselves, but to believe implicitly and in the lump, all that the holy Church believed, and to do whatever their priests enjoined them, without making any inquiries; and this, they declared, was the way to be good Christians.

Now to waive the question how far any one is *likely* to lead a moral life who knows little or nothing about his religion—let it be supposed that a man is leading such a life; still I contend that it cannot be said to be a Christian life, if it does not spring from Christian principles. The brute-animals conform to the design of their Maker, and act in a manner suitable to the nature with which He has endued them: but it would sound strange to say that they are *religious*. Why not? because they have no knowledge or notion of a God, but fulfil his designs without intending and without knowing it. And no more can a man be said to embrace the Christian religion, and to lead a Christian life, who does indeed fulfil all the Christian commandments, but not from any Christian principle—from any motives peculiar to the Christian religion—but for the sake of credit, or health, or prosperity, in the world, or from fear of human punishment— or from deference to the authority of the Priest, or of some other person whom he looks up to, or from any other such motive. Worldly goods will undoubtedly be produced by honest industry, temperance, friendliness, and good conduct in general. And it is conceivable therefore, (I do not say likely,) but it is certainly conceivable, that a man might conduct himself practically as a Christian should do, merely for the sake of these worldly advantages, and not from any Christian principle. But in that case his could no more be called a Christian life, than that of a brute-animal, or than the movements of a machine. The patient who has been cured of his disease, by strictly conforming to the directions of a skilful physician, is not, by swallowing the medicines prescribed, a step the nearer to becoming himself a physician[q].

Every part of the New Testament bears witness

---

[q] See Arist. Eth. Nic. b. ii. ch. 4. b. vi. ch. 12.

to the truth of what I have been saying. The apostles do not even allow it to be sufficient, that a man should believe in Christianity, without knowing *why* he believes it. "Be always ready," says the apostle Paul, "to give a reason for the hope that is in you." Indeed it is plain, that if any one believes any thing without any reason, but merely because some one has told him to do so, even if that which he believes be the truth, yet it is only by chance that he believes the truth;—he does not believe it *because* it is true; and this is not faith, but blind credulity. Now "without faith it is impossible to please God." And, according to the apostles, the Christian is required not only to believe in his religion, and to know what that religion is, but to implant in his mind Christian feelings and motives—" to grow in *grace*," as well as " in the *knowledge* of our Lord Jesus Christ"—to be actuated by gratitude and love for Christ, who died for his sins—by an earnest desire to prove that love by copying his example—by obeying his commands—by being led by his Spirit; and, at every step he takes, "looking unto Jesus the Author and Finisher of our faith," as his pattern and his support in this life, and his eternal rewarder in the next.

Such being then the view which Christ himself and his apostles took of the Christian religion, which religion he evidently meant to be " preached to every creature," and considered as one which might be, and should be, embraced by men of all classes, it is plain, that, if they were not mistaken in their views—in short, if they really were sent from God—it is possible and needful that all classes should have a sufficiency of education to enable them to understand what their religion is, and why it should be received, and how it is to be acted upon.

It is but a slight modification of the same Romanist-principle to propose that the poor should indeed be taught to read, and should have the *four Evangelists* put into their hands, but that all, except learned divines, should be discouraged as much as possible from the perusal of the *Apostolic Epistles*, lest they should " wrest these to their own destruction;" a pretext which was urged with equal reason, and perhaps with more consistency, by the Romanists, for precluding the people from reading " the other Scriptures" also[q].

[q] I have treated fully of this question in Essay ii. Second Series.

The Christian religion, as represented in Scripture, is one that is to be believed on rational conviction, and studied, and felt, and brought into the practice of life, by each man for himself, in all classes of society. The Christian religion, as perverted by the Church of Rome, and as human nature is always tending to pervert it, is in fact *two* religions; one for the initiated few, and one for the mass of the people, who are to follow implicitly the guidance of the others, trusting to their vicarious wisdom, and piety, and learning, believing and practising just as much as these permit and require.

Perhaps the use of the terms " pastor" and " flock," to express the relation between the minister and his congregation, may have led the incautious to form insensibly a notion of some more close analogy than really subsists. He cannot too often or too earnestly warn the people, that they are not properly *his* flock, but Christ's; he is only an Assistant and Servant of the " Chief Shepherd;" and must not only refer at every step to Scripture, but also warn his hearers not to take upon trust his interpretation, but themselves to " search the Scriptures daily, whether those things be so" which he teaches. The language of Scripture is, (I believe invariably,) "feed the *flock of Christ;*" "feed *my* sheep," &c.

But the Romish system makes the people altogether the priest's flock, by exalting him into the Mediator between them and God. Hence sprung the doctrine of the necessity of Confession to a priest, and of the efficacy of the Penance he may enjoin, and the Absolution he bestows—hence the Celibacy of the Clergy, as of an Order of men of peculiar sanctity. Hence the doctrine of works of Supererogation, and of the supposed transferableness from one man to another of the merit of such extraordinary holiness as is not required of Christians in general.

§. 9. I repeat, that these, and a whole train of similar absurdities, are too gross to have been forced upon the belief of men not predisposed to receive them:—predisposed, I mean, not by mere intellectual weakness, but by a moral perversity combined with it;—by a heart alienated from God, yet fearful of his displeasure, and coveting the satisfaction of a quiet conscience at the least possible expence of personal piety and personal exertion.

In all ages and countries, man, through the disposition he inherits from our first parents, is more desirous of a *quiet* and approving, than of a vigilant and *tender*, conscience;—studious to escape the *thought* of spiritual danger, more than the danger itself; and to induce, at any price, some one to assure him confidently that he is safe—to " prophesy unto him smooth things," and to " speak peace," even " when there is no peace."

Inexcusable indeed, in the sight of God, are those who encourage and take advantage of such a delusion; but the people have little right to complain of them. To many of them one might say, " you have had what you sought; you were not seeking in sincerity to know and to please God; if you had been, you would have perceived the vanity of attempting to substitute the piety and good works of a sinful fellow-mortal for your own; you would have perceived the extravagance of imagining that you could purchase happiness or relief in a future state, by hiring a priest to say masses for your soul: what you sought for in reality, was the repose of your soul in this life; a security from the disturbances of conscience, and from a sense of personal responsibility: these false comforts are what in reality your heart was set on; and these alone are what you have purchased."

If such then be the natural propensity of the human mind, we must expect that it will always, and every where, be struggling to shew itself, not only when encouraged, but when not carefully watched and repressed, by the ministry.

I might appeal to any one who has had, and has made use of, the requisite experience, whether he has not continually met with more or less of this tendency to substitute the religious knowledge, the faith—the piety—the prayers—the holiness and purity, of the Minister, for that of the Layman.

How many are there that regard the study of the Scriptures, and the endeavour to understand them, as a professional pursuit, very becoming to a clergyman, but of which little or nothing is required of the laity;—that speak of all the peculiar doctrines of Christianity under the title of " theological mysteries," with which the clergy may suitably be occupied, but with which it is needless, if not even presumptuous and profane, for the unlearned to concern themselves;—that regard the practice of family-devotions as very proper in the house of a clergyman, but in any other, as uncalled for, or even savouring of pharisaical ostentation. Nay, even licentious or profane discourse, intemperance and debauchery, or devotedness to frivolous amusements, we often hear characterised as " unbecoming a clergyman," in a sort of tone which implies the speaker's feeling to be, that they are unbecoming merely to a *clergyman*, not, to a Christian.

§. 10. Many things again there are, which, being considered as in themselves indifferent, are not necessarily unsuitable to a Christian as such, but of which some are regarded by a greater, and some by a smaller number, as professionally unsuited to a Minister of religion. Now it might perhaps have been expected, that the views, as to this point, of different persons among the laity, should correspond respectively with the different views they take of their own obligations; I mean, that those who are the less, or the more, scrupulous as to their own conduct, should allow a greater, or a less, latitude to the clergy in respect of the professional strictness of life and seriousness of demeanour required of *them*. But experience shews that this is very often the reverse of the fact. None are more rigid in exacting of clergymen not only purity of life, but the most unbending seriousness of deportment, and abstinence from almost every kind of amusement, than many of those, who, in their own lives, are the most unrestrained in the pursuit of amusement, and who exhibit the greatest degree of frivolity or of worldliness in their pursuits—of levity in their conversation, and of inattention to religious subjects. Does not this imply a lurking tendency to that very error which has been openly sanctioned and established in the Romish Church? the error of thinking to serve God by a deputy and representative;—of substituting *respect* for religion and its ministers, for personal religion;—and regarding the learning and faith, the prayer and piety, and the scrupulous sanctity, of the priest, as being in some way or other efficaciously transferred from him to the people. It seems some consolation to such persons as I am alluding to that they have *heard* sound doctrine at least, if they have not laid it to heart; that they have *witnessed* and *respected* a strict and unblemished life, and a serious deportment, though they have not copied it; and that on their death-bed they will be enabled to send for a minister of undoubted learning and piety, and enjoy the benefit of his prayers and his blessing, though the holy water and the Extreme-Unction of the Romanists have been laid aside. They take little care indeed to keep their own lights burning; but when summoned to meet their Lord, they will have one to whom they may apply in their extremity, saying, " Give us of your oil, for our lamps are going out."

All indeed, who are in any degree under such a delusion as I am describing, are not subject to it in the *same* degree; but attentive observation will convince every candid enquirer, that in this, as well as in other points, mankind are naturally and generally Romanists in heart;—predisposed, by the tendencies of their original disposition, to errors substantially the same with those which are embodied in the Romish system.

But are not, it may be urged, ignorance of religion and unchristian conduct, much more censurable in the ministers of religion than in others? The answer is, that this is a point for *them* to consider. Of every one the more is required in proportion as the more is given—in proportion as his opportunities may have been greater, and his temptations less, than his neighbour's; but this is a matter for him, not for his neighbour, to be occupied upon. Let each class of men, and each individual man, think chiefly of improving the talent committed to himself; remembering, that even the mote in his own eye, is more his concern than the beam that is in his brother's. It is for the clergy to meditate on their own peculiar and deep responsibility: it is for the laity to consider, not how much more is expected of others, but how much, of themselves.

But again, should there, it may be said, be no professional difference in habits of life between the clergy and the laity?

There should: for, in the first place, as religious *teachers*, they may be expected to be more especially occupied in fitting themselves for that office; in qualifying themselves to *explain*, and to *enforce* on others, the evidences, the doctrines, and the obligations of religion; but they are not to be expected to understand more of things surpassing human reason, than God has made known by revelation, or to be the *depositaries* of certain mysterious speculative doctrines; but "*stewards* of the mysteries of God," rightly dividing or dispensing (ὀρθοτομοῦντες) the word of truth."

And in respect of their general habits of life and deportment, undoubtedly they should consider, that not only of every profession, but of each age, sex, and condition in life, something characteristic is fairly expected in regard to matters in themselves indifferent. The same things are not decorous or indecorous, in a magistrate, and a private person—in a young, and an old man, in those of the higher, and of the lower, orders of society, in a man, and in a woman, or in persons of different professions. And each man's own discretion must determine how he is to conduct himself in respect of things intrinsically indifferent, so as to preserve the decorum of his own peculiar situation, as distinct from another's, without giving needless offence, or in any other way producing ill effects, on either side.

§. 11. For there *are* dangers on *both* sides; and with one brief remark on a danger not unfrequently overlooked, I will dismiss the present subject.

It is I believe sometimes supposed by some of the best-intentioned among the ministry, that there is little or no danger except on the side of laxity;—that excessive scrupulosity in respect of matters in themselves indifferent can, at the worst, only be unnecessary. Of course it will not be expected that I should enter into particulars, or attempt to draw the line in each case that may occur: but the remark to which I would invite attention is, that as it is confessedly one great part of a clergyman's duty to set a good *example*, so, it is self-evident that his example can have no influence—(except on his brother-ministers)—no chance of being imitated by the People, in respect of any thing which he is supposed to do or to abstain from, merely *as* a clergyman. Whatever things they are which are supposed to be *professionally* decorous or indecorous—whatever is supposed to be suitable or unsuitable to a clergyman as such, and not to Christians as Christians—it is plain that no strictness, on the part of the clergy, in these points, can have the least tendency to induce a corresponding strictness in the laity. I am not saying that there *are* no points of this nature;—that there should be *nothing* peculiar belonging to the clergy; but merely that in these points they are setting no *example* to the people;—that *that* in short is not an example, which is supposed peculiar to one profession, and therefore not meant to be imitated in others. I admit that a life of great strictness in such points, may give great satisfaction—may be admired—may procure respect for the individual, and so far, may even give weight to what he says on other points; nay, it may be even called by the unthinking *exemplary;* but it is plain, that, so far as it is regarded as *professional*, it never can *be* exemplary, except to the clergy themselves.

And the more there is of this professional distinction, the greater will be the danger, and the more sedulously must it be guarded against, of the people's falling into the error of regarding other things also as pertaining to the Christian Minister alone, which in fact pertain to the Christian: the longer the list is of things forbidden or enjoined to the clergy and not to the laity, the greater the risk of their adding to the list that Christian knowledge, that Christian spirit and temper, and that Christian self-control and sobriety of conduct, which are required of all that partake of the Christian covenant and Christian hopes[r].

Not only therefore must the clergy be blameless in the performance of *their* duties, but they must carefully distinguish *which* of them are their duties as *Christians*, and *which*, merely as *ministers;* and with that view they must avoid unnecessarily multiplying professional distinctions; lest the most unimpeachable conduct should fail to convey an example, from its being supposed not designed for imitation.

[r] " Absurd as the thought is when expressed in words, man would be virtuous, be humane, be charitable, *by proxy,* &c." *Letter to Mr. Peel, on Pauperism*, p. 19.

How far I am indebted to this work for the first suggestion of many of the principles I have endeavoured to develop in the present chapter, is more than I can distinctly pronounce: especially as the Author is one who has more or less contributed, directly or indirectly, to the formation of nearly all my opinions on the most important points.

We cannot indeed be too learned in " the mysteries of the kingdom of heaven," and in the knowledge of " all the counsel of God," or too scrupulous in our conformity to his will: but then only can we be " pure from the blood of all men," if we " set before *them* all the counsel of God"—make *known* to *them* " the mystery of the Gospel," and their " *fellowship* in that mystery"—and lead them to apply practically their religious knowledge, and to be " followers of us, even as we are of Christ Jesus."

CHAPTER III.

PIOUS FRAUDS.

§. 1. It may be said of almost all the Romish errors, that they not only have their common source in man's frail nature, but also are so intimately connected together, that they will generally be found, if not directly to generate, yet mutually to foster and promote, one another. For example, the disposition already noticed, to speculate concerning superhuman mysteries unconnected with practice, though it does not alone produce, yet favours and encourages, the error of reserving one portion of faith and piety for a superior initiated class, and making *their* religion a vicarious substitute for that of the people, who are to trust in and implicitly follow the direction of their guide. And this corruption again, though it does not directly engender, yet fosters and increases another; that of maintaining this spiritual tyranny, by *deceit*. Those who have once adopted the system of keeping the vulgar in partial darkness, will easily reconcile themselves to the practice of misleading them, where it seems needful, by false lights. From a conviction of the necessity of keeping them in implicit subjection to their authority, the transition is easy to the maintenance of that authority, by what are regarded as salutary delusions.

It is not however to any deliberate scheme of an ambitious hierarchy that this branch of priestcraft owes its origin; nor is it indeed properly *priest*craft. The tendency to resort to deceit for the compassing of *any* end whatever that seems hardly attainable by honest means, and not least, if it be supposed a good end, is inherent, if any fault be inherent, in our corrupt nature. And in each age and country instances occur of this offence, such as perhaps in a different age and country appear so monstrous as to be hardly credible, from the difficulty of estimating aright the peculiar circumstances which in each instance constituted the temptation.

And this is more peculiarly the case, when those who are passing judgment on any instance of fraud, chance to regard that as a *bad* end which the authors of the fraud pursued as a good one;—when they are convinced of the falsity of the conclusion, which was perhaps sincerely held, by those who sought to support it by deceitful means. For example, the fraud related to have been practised by the Jewish rulers in reference to our Lord's resurrection, seems at first sight almost to surpass the limits of human impudence and wickedness in imposture. "And when they were assembled with the elders, they gave large money unto the soldiers, saying, Say ye, His disciples came by night and stole Him away while we slept[a]." But let it be remembered, that the deceit here recorded, must certainly be referred to the class of what are called, "Pious Frauds:" those, namely, which any one employs and justifies to himself, as conducing, according to his view, to the defence or promotion of true religion. There is in such conduct a union of sincerity and insincerity—of conscientiousness in respect of the end, and unscrupulous dishonesty as to the means: for without the one of these ingredients there could be no *fraud;* and with-

[a] Matt. xxviii. 12, 13.

out the other, it could in no sense be termed a *pious* fraud.

And such, I say, undoubtedly was the fraud we are considering. For the Jewish elders certainly did not believe in Jesus as the Messiah, though they could not deny his superhuman powers. There is hardly any evidence which a man may not bring himself to resist, if it come, not before, but after, he has fully made up his mind. But in the present instance the established belief in magic, and the agency of demons in subjection to those skilled in the art, furnished a better evasion than could be devised among *us*, of the force of the evidence offered. And being predetermined by their own view of the ancient prophecies, to reject the claim of Jesus, they pronounced Him (as the unbelieving Jews do at this day[b]) to be a powerful Magician, and one

---

[b] A book is now extant and well known among the Jews, which gives this account of Him: and it furnishes a striking confirmation of the statement of the Evangelists; viz. that the unbelieving Jews of his days did admit his miraculous powers. For the book must have been compiled from traditions afloat in the nation; and it is utterly inconceivable that, if those who were contemporary with our Lord, and on the spot, had

who " deceived the people." As maintainers therefore of the Mosaic law, in whose divine authority they were believers, they held themselves not only authorized, but bound, to suppress his religion: according to our Lord's own prophecy, " Whosoever killeth you, will think that he doeth God service." For the prevention therefore of the mischief they apprehended, " lest all men should believe in Him, and the Romans should come, and take away their place and nation," (an event which, it is remarkable, did actually take place in consequence of their rejecting Him, and trusting to false Christs,) they scrupled not to resort to falsehood, to weaken the effect of his miracles.

The benefit derivable from such an example as this is apt to be lost to us, from our dwelling exclusively on the badness of the object these men pursued; and not enough considering, abstractedly from that, the profligacy of the means employed. Persuaded as we are that Jesus was

---

denied the fact of the miracles, any tradition should afterwards have sprung up, *admitting* the miracles, and accounting for them by the hypothesis of Magic.

the true Messiah, we are apt, in contemplating the perversity of those who closed their eyes against the evidence of this, to blend in our minds, *that* sin, with the other, which is quite distinct—the *fraud* with which Christianity was opposed;—to mix up, and connect in our thoughts, as they were connected in fact, the rejection of the Son of God, and the falsification of the evidence of his resurrection;—and, in short, almost to forget that if Jesus had been indeed a deceiver, that would not have justified the employment of deceit to maintain God's cause against Him.

In proportion as feelings of this kind prevail, the benefit of such an example to ourselves is destroyed. Our abhorrence of their sin has no tendency to fortify us against temptation;—against that temptation, I mean, in the very nature of which it is implied that the end proposed is sincerely believed to be good. Whether this belief chance to be correct or not, a just estimate of the heinousness of what is properly denominated pious fraud, would lead us to regard it with equal detestation, whether employed in a good or in a bad cause.

§. 2. The tendency to take this indistinct view of things—to contemplate in confused conjunction a bad end, and wrong means employed to support it, has doubtless contributed to prevent Protestants from deriving the benefit they might, in the way of example and warning, from the errors of the Romanists. In our abhorrence of the frauds they have so often employed in support of their corrupt system, we are prone perhaps to forget, or at least not sufficiently to consider, that it is not the corruptness of the system that makes the frauds detestable; and that the same sin may no less easily beset ourselves, and will be no less offensive to God, however sound may be our own system of faith. With a view to keep this more steadily before the mind, I have limited my remarks to the subject of what are called *pious* frauds, because it is against these alone that we have need to be put on our guard. It would be vain to admonish an unbelieving hypocrite: but a sincere Protestant Christian may need to be reminded, that as he believes his own religion to be true, so do many of the Romanists believe theirs; and that though they are in fact erroneous in this belief, it is not *that erroneousness* that either leads them to resort to pious frauds, or exposes them to just censure for so doing; nor consequently, can the correctness of his own faith secure him from the danger, or extenuate the guilt, of practising a like deceit.

I have dwelt thus earnestly on a truth which, though perpetually overlooked in practice, is self-evident the moment it is stated, because the mistake opposed to it is closely connected with, or rather is a part of, that which it has been my principal object throughout the present work to counteract;—the mistake, I mean, of referring various errors of Romanism to the Romish Church, as their source—of representing that system as the cause of those corruptions which in fact produced it, and which have their origin in our common nature: and hence of regarding what are emphatically called, the errors of Romanism, as peculiar to that Church, and into which, consequently, Protestants are in no danger of falling. But all of them, as I have already endeavoured in some instances to point out, may be traced up to the evil propensities of human nature: and the one now under consideration, no less than the rest. The tendency to aim at a supposed good end by fraudulent means, is not peculiar to the members of the Romish Church;—it is not peculiar to those who are *mistaken* in their belief as to what *is* a good end;—it is not peculiar to any sect, age, or country;—it is not peculiar to any *subject-matter*, religious or secular, but is the spontaneous growth of the corrupt soil of man's heart.

Protestants, however, are apt to forget this: and it is often needful to remind them, and only to remind them, (for detailed proof is unnecessary,) that frauds of this kind are every where, and always have been, prevalent;—that the heathen legislators and philosophers, for instance, encouraged, or connived at, a system of popular mythology which they disbelieved, with a view to the public good—for the sake of maintaining among the vulgar, through fear of the gods, and expectations of Elysium and Tartarus, a conformity to those principles of rectitude whose authority they sincerely acknowledged, though on grounds totally unconnected with religion. Their statesmen deluded and overawed the populace with prodigies and oracles, not much less than the Romish priesthood. Nor has the Greek Church, or the other Eastern Churches, always independent as they have been of the Church of Rome, and generally hostile to her, fallen much short of her in this and indeed in most of her other abominations.

The temptation indeed to deceive, either positively or negatively, i. e. either by introducing, or by tolerating error, is one of the strongest that assail our frail nature, in cases where the conscience is soothed by our having in view what we believe to be a good end, and where that end seems hardly attainable but by fraudulent means. For the path of falsehood, though in reality slippery and dangerous, will often be the most obvious, and seemingly the shortest. Accordingly nothing is more common, among the indolent and thoughtless, when entrusted with the management of children, than to resort to this compendious way of controlling them; for the employment of deceit with those who are so easily deceived, will often serve a present turn much better than scrupulous veracity; though at the expence of tenfold ultimate inconvenience [c].

[c] Mrs. Hoare's Hints on Early Education.

§. 3. The tendency then to this partial dishonesty—towards the justification of fraudulent means by the supposed goodness of the object—being so deeply rooted in man's nature, found its way, of course, along with the other corruptions incident to humanity, into the Romish Church. And it was fostered by those other corruptions; especially, as has been already remarked, by that one which was treated of in the preceding chapter; the drawing, namely, of an unduly strong line of separation between the priesthood and the laity; so as to constitute almost two distinct kinds of Christianity for the two classes, whereof the one were by some superior sanctity and knowledge to compensate for the deficiencies of the other, and to be not only their spiritual directors, but in some sort their substitutes in the service of the Deity.

When it was understood that the Monastic Orders, and the clergy, in general, were to be regarded as persons initiated into certain sacred mysteries, withheld from the vulgar—as professing a certain distinct and superior description of Christianity—and as guides whom the great mass of Christians were to trust implicitly, it naturally followed, that the knowledge of Scripture was considered, first, as unnecessary, and next, as unfit, for the generality: and it was equally natural to proceed from the suppression of knowledge to the toleration first, and then to the encouragement and propagation, of superstitious errors among the multitude. There is (as I formerly observed) a craving in ignorant minds after the delusions of superstition: and this it was thought reasonable to indulge, in the case of those whom it was supposed impossible or improper to enlighten. Incapable as they were reckoned, and as they *consequently became*, of believing in their religion on rational and solid evidence, or of being kept in the paths of Christian duty by the highest and purest Christian principles, it seemed necessary to let their faith and their practice strike root, as it were, in the artificial soil of idle legends about miracles wrought by holy relics, and at the intercession of saints—in the virtues of holy water, Extreme Unction, and the like.

How far, in each particular instance, any one, whether of the Romish or of any other persuasion, who propagates and connives at any error, may be himself deceived, or may be guilty of pious *fraud;*—and how far his fraud, if it be such, may be properly a *pious* fraud, i. e. designed to promote what he sincerely believes to be a good end, or, on the other hand, may be carried on from interested or ambitious views—all this can of course be thoroughly known to none but the Searcher of hearts. It is highly probable, however, that most of these persons have *begun* in wilful deceit, and advanced more and more towards superstitious *belief.* Indeed it is matter of common remark, that those who have long repeated a falsehood, often bring themselves at length to credit it. The very curse sent on those who do not love the truth, is that of " a strong delusion that they should believe a lie." And thus, in the present instance, when any one is eagerly bent on the pursuit of a certain end, he will commonly succeed in persuading himself in time, first, that it is a pious and good end—then, that it is justifiable to promote it by tolerating or inculcating what is false—and lastly, that that very falsehood is truth. Many a one, it is to be feared, gives himself credit for being conscientious, who is so indeed in one sense of the word, but in this sense only, not that he is, properly speaking, led by his conscience, but that he himself leads his conscience;—that he has persevered in what is wrong, till he has at length convinced himself that it is right.

§. 4. That intermediate state however, between complete hypocrisy and complete self-delusion—that state which gives rise to what are properly called pious frauds—is probably much more common than either of the extremes. Those, for instance, who opposed the Reformation, were probably most of them neither worldly-minded hypocrites altogether indifferent about true religion, nor, on the other hand, sincere believers in the justice of all the claims of the Romish see which they supported, and in the truth of all the Romish doctrines which they maintained; but men who were content to submit to *some* injustice, and to connive at some error, rather than risk, in the attempt to reform abuses, the overthrow of all religion. They preferred an edifice, which, though not faultless, they considered highly serviceable, to the apprehended alternative of a heap of ruins. And accordingly they made up their minds to profess and maintain the whole of what they only partially believed and approved, and to defend by falsehood those portions of the fortification which they perceived were left open by truth.

We of this day are perhaps not disposed to do justice to many of the actors in those times. *We* know by experience, that the Reformation did not lead to the universal destruction of religion; and we know that most of the confusion and other evils which did result, and of which the effects are not yet done away, are attributable to the obstinacy with which the others persisted in maintaining every abuse, and the discredit they brought on religion in general, by the employment of falsehood and subterfuge in her defence. We are apt to suppose, therefore, that the apprehensions which the event did not realize, must have been either utterly extravagant and childish, or else altogether feigned, by men, who in reality had an interest in the maintenance of abuses, and introduced their fears for religion as a mere pretext. For in studying history, those portions of it especially which are to us the most interesting, which are precisely those in which the *results* are before our eyes and familiar to us from childhood, this very circumstance is apt to make us unfair judges of the actors, and thus to prevent us from profiting as we might, by their examples. We are apt, I mean, to forget, how probable many things might appear, which we know did not take place; and to regard as perfectly chimerical, expectations which we know were not realized, but which, had we lived in those times, we should doubtless ourselves have entertained; and to imagine that there was no *danger* of those evils which were in fact escaped. We are apt also to make too little allowance for prejudices and associations of ideas, which no longer exist precisely in the same form, among ourselves, but which are perhaps not more at variance with right reason than others with which ourselves are infected.

From the earliest down to the latest periods of history, these causes impede the full and clear, and consequently profitable, view of the transactions related. In respect of the very earliest of all human transactions, it is matter of common remark how prone many are to regard with mingled wonder, contempt, and indignation, the transgression of our first parents; as if they were not a fair sample of the human race;—as if any of us would not, if he had been placed in precisely the same circumstances, have acted as they did. The Corinthians, probably, had perused with the same barren wonder the history of the backslidings of the Israelites; and needed that Paul should remind them, that these things were written for their example and admonition. And all, in almost every portion of history, they read, have need of a corresponding warning, to endeavour to fancy themselves the persons they read of, that they may recognize in the accounts of past times, the portraiture of their own. It is by a strong effort of a vivid *imagination* (a faculty whose importance *in the study of history*, is seldom thought of) that we can so far transport ourselves in idea, to the period, for instance, of the Reformation, or to any period anterior to it, as to forget for the moment all our actual knowledge of the results— to put ourselves completely in the place of the persons living in those times, and to enter fully into all their feelings.

In proportion as we succeed in this effort, we shall feel more and more strongly how awfully alarming must have been the first struggles of opposition to the existing system—how total a subversion of all religion, and dissolution of all the ties of social order, the first innovations must have appeared to threaten; and how little most men must have been able to foresee or conjecture at what point the tendency to change, if permitted to proceed, could be expected to stop. And we shall then, I think, cease to wonder, that the frailty of our common nature should have led conscientious men (conscientious, I mean, as far as regards the goodness, in their opinion, of the *end* proposed) to use without scruple almost any means, whether of force or fraud, to maintain the existing system, and to avert what appeared to them such frightful dangers.

§. 5. What we should learn for our own use from such a view is, not that the dishonest artifices of Romanism should stand excused in our eyes, but that we should estimate aright their temptations, in order the better to understand our own—that we should consider human nature as not having been then, in so excessive a degree as we are apt to fancy, worse than it is now;— and that we should condemn their frauds, not as employed to support a bad system, and to avert imaginary evils—since to them, perhaps, the system appeared as good as our own does to us, and the evils as real as any that we apprehend appear in our eyes—but from the general inexpediency of fraud—from its intrinsic turpitude, and from its especial unfitness to be employed in a sacred cause. Considerations, such as these, will set us upon a more painful, but more profitable, task, than that of judging our ancestors and our erring brethren—the task of examining our own conduct, with a watchful suspicion of the corruption of our own nature, and a lively consciousness of our liability to like temptations with those to which others have yielded. The erroneousness of their views, and the soundness of our own, as to the *end* proposed, does not lessen to us the danger, or the evil, of promoting that end by *means* inconsistent with perfect integrity.

To any one who should be disposed not only to *approve* of such a vigilant and severe self-examination as has been recommended, but also earnestly and systematically to put it in practice, it may be worth while to suggest the remark, that what may be suitably called pious frauds, fall naturally into the two classes of *positive* and *negative;* the one, the introduction or propagation of what is false; the other, the mere toleration of it—the connivance at any kind of mistake or delusion already existing in men's minds. Again, in another point of view, frauds may be regarded, either as having relation, on the one hand, to fallacious arguments—to false *reasons* for right conclusions—or, on the other hand, to false *doctrines* and erroneous practices, when such are taught or connived at. I have suggested both of these two divisions, as having a reference to practice; because *in* practice it is found that the temptation is stronger (because less alarming to the conscience) to the use of false reasons and sophistical argument in the cause of truth, than to the inculcation or toleration of erroneous doctrine; and again, that there is, for the same reason, a stronger temptation to *negative* than to *positive* fraud; the conscience being easily soothed by the reflection, " this or that is a false notion indeed, but I did not introduce it; and it would unsettle men's minds too much, were I to attempt to undeceive them."

To particularize the several points in which

we of the present day are especially open to temptations of the description I have alluded to, would be a task of much difficulty and delicacy. For if a few cases were selected and dwelt on, (and more than a very few it would be impossible to discuss within any reasonable limits,) some might suppose that it was to these particular cases the whole argument had been directed; and might join issue, as it were, on the question, whether these were such as to bear out that argument: and if something brought forward as an instance of an error, should chance to be such, as by some was sincerely believed—by others had never been heard of—and by others again was regarded as perfectly insignificant—the result might be, that the argument and remarks intended to be *illustrated* by such instances, (if supposed to *rest* on those instances,) might be regarded by some as frivolous, or as unsound. Such at least is the mistake which is not unfrequently made in many subjects; an instance brought forward in illustration of any general remarks or arguments, being not unfrequently regarded as the basis on which the whole depends. And yet, if a physician, for instance, were to be found mistaken in assigning some particular disorder to this or that patient, it would be thought strange to infer from this that no such disorder ever existed.

§. 6. Such, however, being the difficulties in the present subject, it will be better perhaps to abstain from any statement of matters of fact, and to touch briefly, for illustration's sake, on a few *conceivable* cases; which, whether they ever actually occurred or not, will be equally intelligible, and will equally answer the purpose of explanation.

I. For example, it is well known, that there are sects and other parties of Christians, of whose system it forms a part to believe in immediate, sensible, inspiration—that the preachers are directly and perceptibly moved to speak by the Holy Spirit, and utter what He suggests. Now suppose any one, brought up in these principles, and originally perhaps a sincere believer in his own inspiration, becoming afterwards so far sobered, as to perceive, or strongly suspect, their delusiveness, and so to modify, at least, his views of the subject, as in fact to nullify all the *peculiarity* of the doctrine, which yet many of his hearers, he knows, hold in its full extent; must he not be strongly tempted to keep up what will probably seem to him so salutary a delusion? Such a case as this I cannot think to be even of rare occurrence. For a man of sound judgment, and of a reflective turn, must, one would think, have it forced on his attention, that he speaks better after long *practice*, than when a novice— better on a subject he has been *used* to preach on, than on a comparatively new one—and better with *premeditation*, than on a sudden; and all this, as is plain both from the nature of the case, and from Scripture, is inconsistent with inspiration. Practice and study cannot improve the immediate suggestions of the Holy Ghost; and the apostles were on that ground expressly forbidden to " take thought beforehand what they should say, or to premeditate; because it should be *given them* in the same hour what they should say." Again, he will perhaps see cause to alter his views of some passages of Scripture he may have referred to, or in other points to modify some of the opinions he may have expressed; and this again is inconsistent with the idea of inspiration, at least on *both* occasions.

Yet with these views of his own preaching, as not really and properly inspired and infallible, he is convinced that he is inculcating the great and important truths of Christianity—that he is consequently, in a certain sense, under the guidance of the Holy Spirit, from whom all good things must proceed—and that his preaching is of great benefit to his hearers; who yet would cease to attend to it, were he distinctly to declare to them his own real sentiments. In such a case, he must be very strongly tempted to commit the pious fraud of conniving at a belief which he does not himself sincerely hold; consoling perhaps his conscience with the reflection, that when he professes to be moved by the Spirit, he says what he is convinced is true, though *not true in the sense* in which most of his hearers understand it;—not true in the sense which constitutes that very peculiarity of doctrine wherein originated the separation of his sect from other Christians.

II. Again, let us imagine, for example, such an instance as this; that an uneducated person describes to us his satisfaction at having met with a stratum of marine shells on the top of a hill, which he concludes to have been deposited there by the Mosaic deluge, and which afford him a consolatory proof of the truth of the Old Testament history; suppose too he congratulates himself on having satisfied, by this argument, the minds of some sceptics among his own class: what would be our duty, and what would be our conduct, in such a case? to run the apparent risk of not only mortifying his feelings, but shaking his faith, by informing him, (supposing the case such,) that it is fully ascertained that this deposit could not have taken place by the action of such a deluge as Moses describes? or to leave him in full reliance on an argument, which, though unsound, leads him to a true conclusion? This, which is a case conceivably occurring in a Protestant country, seems to me an exact parallel to a multitude of those in which the Romanists practise the negative pious fraud of leaving men under what they suppose a useful delusion.

III. Again, suppose the case of one who should be warmly attached to the religious community of which we are members, in opposition to sectaries, and a regular frequenter of our public worship, in consequence of the mention he finds in Scripture of the *Church*, together with the circumstance, that the building in which we assemble for divine service is called a "Church." No one, who has been much conversant with the uneducated part of society, will doubt the possible existence, at least, of such confusion of thought, though he may not have actually met with it. Now this again is an instance of a just conclusion and right practice founded on a futile reason. Is it not conceivable, that some who would be ashamed to employ such an argument themselves, might yet be tempted to leave it uncontradicted, from a doubt of being able to substitute a sound one, which should be, to that individual, equally satisfactory?

IV. Again, let us imagine a case of some one desirous to receive, and induce others to receive, the rite of Confirmation, from supposing it alluded to, and enjoined, in the passage of Scripture which describes an apostle as going through a certain region "confirming the Churches" (ἐπιστηρίζων); should we venture to attempt removing his conviction from this false basis, and replacing it on a sound one?

V. Suppose again, that some one was conscientiously desirous of receiving this rite, whom the minister could not bring to comprehend the nature of it, or to understand any thing of the baptismal covenant which is renewed before the Christian congregation, and recalled by it, might there not, in such a case, be a seeming danger; that if under such circumstances he refused to sign a recommendation to the Bishop, there might grow up a neglect of the ordinance of Confirmation? while, on the other hand, he would know that his signature would be understood to testify the existence of such fitness on the part of the candidate as in fact was wanting; and that consequently he would be virtually setting his hand to a falsehood; and would, moreover, be encouraging that superstitious notion of some mystical virtue in a rite of which the recipient did not understand the meaning. Now such a case as this, I think, will hardly be considered as inconceivable, or even improbable.

VI. Suppose, again, an individual of the same class to have a deep reverence for the Lord's-day, without even knowing that it *is* the *Lord's*-day, but from supposing Sunday to be the Seventh day of the week, and to be kept holy not with any reference to our Lord's resurrection, but solely in memory of the close of the Creation: there would be, on the one hand, the apparent danger of unsettling his mind, and diminishing his just reverence, by letting him know that it is the First day of the week, and is commemorative of the Resurrection; and, on the other hand, there would be the negative pious fraud of leaving his mistake untouched. "Will ye," says Job, "speak wickedly for God, and talk deceitfully for Him?"

VII. If, again, we should meet with a case of Christians having a deep reverence for all the rites and circumstances of Christian burial, founded on a persuasion that the souls of those whose bodies are interred in consecrated ground, after the performance of the funeral service, are in a more safe state than they would otherwise have been[s], might not a danger be apprehended, of impairing their respect for the ministers of religion and the services of the Church, by inculcating the groundlessness of that persuasion? And might not therefore a minister be tempted,

[s] See Chap. I.

in such a case, to leave undisturbed an error which he could not charge himself with having directly introduced?

VIII. Once more; imagine the case of a man long hardened in irreligious carelessness or gross vices, conscience-stricken on his death-bed, professing sincere repentance, and earnestly wishing for, and seeming to implore, a positive assurance from the minister of his acceptance with God, and his eternal happiness in the next world;— a wish in which the relatives and friends around him should strongly join: and suppose the minister to be one who could not satisfy his own mind that he had any authority in Scripture for speaking positively in such a case; would he not be exposed to a temptation of feigning a confidence he did not feel, for the sake of smoothing the death-bed of one for whom nothing else could be done, and administering comfort to the afflicted survivors?

And if a person so situated were anxious to receive the Eucharist, though he were (suppose) from ignorance respecting religion, and long continuance in careless or depraved habits, combined with the distractions of bodily pain, and the feebleness of mind resulting from disease, utterly incapable of being made to understand the nature of Christian Repentance, or the doctrine of Christian Redemption, or the right use of that Sacrament which he craved for as a kind of magical charm; (with the same kind of superstitious confidence which the Papists place in their Extreme-Unction;) would not the minister be tempted to shut his eyes to the unfitness of such a candidate—to the consequent nullity of the Ordinance, as far as that recipient is concerned—and to the profanation of so celebrating it? And if, moreover, we suppose some fanatical teacher to be at hand ready to make confident promises of salvation if *we* speak doubtfully, and to administer the sacred Ordinance if *we* withhold it—and that he would in that case win many converts, while we should incur odium, as wanting in charity; we must admit that, in such a case as here supposed, the temptation would be very strong, to any but a devoted lover of truth, to connive at error, as the less of the evils before him. And the temptation would be much the stronger both in this and in the other supposed cases, if we imagine them presented to a person who (as might easily be the case) had no distinct perception of the ultimate *dangers* of deceit—of the crowd of errors likely to spring from one—the necessity of supporting hereafter one falsehood by another, to infinity—and the liability to bring truth into discredit by blending it with the untrue; dangers which are recognized in the popular wisdom of appropriate proverbs. These ill consequences may very easily be overlooked in each particular instance: for though it is a just maxim that falsehood is inexpedient in the long run, it is a maxim which it requires no small experience and reach of thought fully and practically to comprehend, and readily to apply: the only safe guide for the great mass of mankind, is the abhorrence of falsehood for its own sake, without looking to its consequences.

Numberless other like instances might be imagined, of, at least conceivable, occurrence in a Protestant country; but those which have been mentioned will be sufficient, if they are admitted to be not, all of them, total impossibilities, to illustrate my meaning;—to shew that our separation from the Church of Rome does not place us (nor can we ever be placed in this life) in a situation which exempts us from all danger of falling into corruptions—among the rest, the justification of pious frauds—substantially similar to those with which that Church is so justly reproached.

As for the cases introduced for the sake of illustration, I must once more protest that they do not profess to be actual facts, but merely conceivable suppositions; and it is not at all my wish that any one should, by testifying displeasure, as against a personal charge, fix on himself the censure brought against a hypothetical case. Indeed I would most gladly be convinced that these and all similar suppositions are not only not agreeable to fact, but are even impossible, and the dangers I apprehend, wholly imaginary. If this be so,

> Why then, my taxing, like a wildgoose, flies
> Unclaimed of any man,

and my warnings will be at least harmless, though unnecessary : " abundans cautela non nocet."

§. 7. I will conclude this chapter with an earnest recommendation of the study (with a view to our own warning and instruction) of the various abuses prevailing in the Romish Church—such a study, I mean, as shall go, not only to ascertain their actual character, but also, to trace their gradual progress from their first appearance, till they became at length embodied in the system, and established as parts of true religion. In many, if not in most instances, they began (as I have formerly observed) with the people; and were at first, many of them, only connived at by the clergy; who dreaded to oppose, or to reform, or to acknowledge, errors, lest they should shake the whole system of faith with which they were connected. And let it not be lost sight of, that the fraud by which they sought to support the system—the " wall daubed with untempered mortar," with which they thought to buttress up the edifice—has always tended to its decay. Not only did it give rise to a hostile separation among Christian Churches, but, in countries which have continued under the papal sway, the abhorrence and contempt excited by the detection of a fraudulent system, has led the far greater part of the educated classes into secret but total apostasy from Christ. With the indiscriminate rashness which is universally so common; they have confusedly blended together in their minds, Christianity, and its corruptions; and having in so many instances detected fraud with absolute certainty, they think it not worth while to inquire further; but take for granted, that all the Church teaches, is one tissue of imposture and superstition throughout.

Let not Protestants, then, lose the benefit of this lesson; " neither let us tempt God, as some of them also tempted;" for " all these things happened unto them for examples, and are written" (if we will but so read them) " for our admonition. Wherefore let him that thinketh he standeth, take heed lest he fall."

CHAPTER IV.

UNDUE RELIANCE ON HUMAN AUTHORITY.

§. 1. THE infallibility of the (so called) Catholic Church, and the substitution of the decrees of Popes or of pretended General Councils, for the Scriptures, as the Christian's rule of faith and practice, is commonly regarded as the foundation of the whole Romish system. And it is so, in this sense, that if it be once admitted, all the rest must follow: if the power of "binding and loosing" belong to the Church of Rome in the extent claimed by her, we have only to ascertain what are her decisions, and to comply with them implicitly.

But I am convinced that this is not the foundation, *historically* considered, of the Romish system;—that the Romish hierarchy did not, in point of fact, first establish their supremacy on a perverted interpretation of certain texts, and then employ the power thus acquired to introduce abuses; but resorted, as occasions led them, to such passages of Scripture as might be wrested to justify the prevailing or growing abuses, and to buttress up the edifice already in great measure reared.

They appeal, as is well known, to our Lord's expression respecting Peter's being made 'the foundation of his Church; an expression which could never by possibility have suggested so extravagant and indeed unmeaning an interpretation as that of a *succession* of men being each a *foundation*[a]: and they also appeal to the declaration [b], " Whatsoever thou shalt bind on earth shall be bound in heaven, and whatsoever thou shalt loose on earth shall be loosed in heaven," as conferring on the Church of Rome the supreme power She claims. Of this and the other corresponding passage in our Lord's discourses, the most probable explanation is that which refers to the language common among the Jewish Doctors; who employed the expressions " to bind," and " to loose," (as may be seen abundantly in their works re-

[a] Hinds's History of the Rise of Christianity, vol. i. p. 9.
[b] Matth. xvi. 19.

specting traditional regulations now extant [c]) in the sense of enacting and abrogating;—establishing any rule or ordinance, so as to make it obligatory or binding—or, on the other, abolishing, or forbearing to enact, some rule, and leaving men exempt—released—loosed—from the observance of it. Our Lord's declaration, therefore, will amount to this;—that the governors in each branch of the Church which He founded—of the Kingdom appointed to his disciples—with whom, and consequently with their successors, He promised to be always even unto the end of the world—that these governors should have power to make regulations for the good government of that society—to admit or refuse admission into it—and to establish such rules as they might think suitable, for the edification of its members, and their decorous worship of God: and that such regulations of Christ's servants on earth, should be ratified and sanctioned by the authority of their unseen and spiritual Master—should be bound in heaven by Him.

It seems no less plain, that to the governors of every Society must be entrusted the duty of

[c] See Wotton on the Misna.

checking such disorderly and scandalous conduct in its members, as goes to interfere with the purposes of its institution, by reprimand or other penalties, and ultimately, in extreme cases, by expulsion: and they must be empowered to remit such penalties, or to readmit an expelled member, on his testifying contrition, and making satisfactory promises of good behaviour. And this is admitted by most Protestants to be the force of that declaration, " whosesoever sins ye remit, they are remitted, and whosesoever sins ye retain, they are retained:" not as if fallible men had power to judge of the *sincerity* of any one's contrition;— or even if they had, could presume to claim the divine privilege of forgiving sins as *against God*;— but that they have power to inflict or remit the penalties of Church-censure, and to exclude, retain, or re-admit, as far as *outward privileges* are concerned, any member of their own branch of the visible Church.

As for the regulations respecting the conduct of members of that Society, which they have power to enact or abrogate, it is obvious, that, as far as these extend only to things in themselves indifferent, (such as festival-days, outward ceremonies, and the like) which may and should vary in different ages and countries, but yet require to be in each instance regulated by *some* acknowledged authority—as far, I say, as this exercise of power is confined to matters not in themselves essential, it may be (and must be, supposing inspiration withdrawn) entrusted to uninspired men. But, on the other hand, the promulgating of such articles of faith and rules of conduct as are intrinsically necessary, and make part of the terms of salvation—that this office—the binding and loosing in respect of things essential—can be left in the hands of none but inspired men, all must allow; and *we* should add, in the hands of men who (like the Apostles) give *proof* of their inspiration, and produce the credentials of their divine commission by working sensible miracles.

§. 2. Whatever slight differences, however, there may be among Protestants as to the precise sense of these passages, and of all that our Lord has said on the subject, they all agree in this; that it will by no means bear the interpretation put on it by the Romanists; who are commonly supposed, as has been above remarked, to derive from their mistaken view of our Lord's expressions in this place, the monstrous doctrines of the Universal Supremacy of the Church of Rome, and her infallibility as to matters of faith. I have said that these doctrines are *supposed* to be thus derived, because there is good reason to think that such is not really the case; and that in this point, as in most of those connected with the peculiarities of Romanism, the mistake is usually committed of confounding cause and effect. When there is any question about any of the doctrines or practices which characterise that Church, it is natural, and it is common, to inquire on what rational arguments or on what Scriptural authority these are made to rest; the reasons adduced are examined, and, if found insufficient, the point is considered as settled: and so it is, as far as regards those particular doctrines or practices, when judged of by an intelligent and unbiassed inquirer. That which is indefensible, *ought* certainly to be abandoned. But it is a mistake, and a very common, and practically not unimportant one, to conclude, that the *origin* of each tenet or practice is to be found in those arguments or texts which are urged in support of it;—that they furnish the cause, on the removal of which the effects will cease of course—and that when once those reasonings are exploded, and those texts rightly explained, all danger is at end of falling into similar errors. The fact is, that in a great number of instances, and by no means exclusively in questions connected with religion, the erroneous belief or practice has arisen first, and the theory has been derived afterwards for its support. Into whatever opinions or conduct men are led by any human propensities, they seek to defend and justify these by the best arguments they can devise; and then, assigning, as they often do, in perfect sincerity, these arguments, as the cause of their adopting such notions, they misdirect the course of our inquiry. And thus the chance (however small it may be at any rate) of rectifying their errors, is diminished. For if these be in reality traceable to some deep-seated principle of our nature, as soon as ever one false foundation on which they have been placed is removed, another will be substituted: as soon as one theory is proved untenable, a new one will be devised in its place. And in the mean time, we ourselves are liable to be lulled into a false security against errors, whose real origin is to be sought in the universal propensities of human nature.

Not only Romanism, but almost every system of superstition, in order to be rightly understood, should be (if I may so speak) read backwards. To take an instance, in illustration of what has been said, from the Mythological system of the Ancients; if we inquire why the rites of sepulture were regarded by them as of such vast importance, we are told, that, according to their system of religious belief, the souls of those whose bodies were unburied were doomed to wander disconsolate on the banks of the river Styx. Such a tenet, supposing it previously established, was undoubtedly well-calculated to produce or increase the feeling in question: but is it not much the more probable supposition, that the natural anxiety about our mortal remains, which has been felt in every age and country, and which those who partake of it are at a loss to explain and justify, drove them to imagine and adopt the theory which gave a rational appearance to feelings and practices already existing?

Again, if the Romanists are urged to defend and explain their practice of praying for the souls of the departed, they refer us to the doctrines of their Church respecting Purgatory. But it is not really the doctrine of Purgatory which led to prayers for the dead; on the contrary, it is doubtless the practice of praying for the dead that gave rise to that doctrine; a doctrine which manifestly savours of having been invented to serve a purpose. Accordingly it never, I believe, found its way into the Greek Church, though prayers for the dead (difficult as it is to justify such a practice on other grounds) has long prevailed in that Church no less than in the Romish.

If, again, we call on the Romanists to justify their invocation of saints, which seems to confer on these the divine attribute of omnipresence, they tell us that the Almighty miraculously reveals to the glorified saints in heaven the prayers addressed to them, and then listens to their intercession in behalf of the supplicants. But the real state of the case, doubtless, is, that the practice which began gradually in popular superstition, and was fostered and sanctioned by the mingled weakness and corruption of the priesthood, was afterwards supported by a theory too unfounded and too extravagantly absurd to have ever obtained a general reception, had it not come in aid of a practice already established, and which could be defended on no better grounds.

And the same principle will apply to the greater part of the Romish errors; the cause assigned for each of them will in general be found to be in reality its effect;—the arguments by which it is supported—to have gained currency from men's partiality for the conclusion. It is thus that we must explain, what is at first sight so great a paradox, the vast difference of effect apparently produced in minds of no contemptible powers, by the same arguments;—the frequent inefficacy of the most cogent reasonings, and the hearty satisfaction with which the most futile are often listened to and adopted. Nothing is, in general, easier than to convince one who is prepared and desirous to be convinced; or to gain any one's full approbation of arguments tending to a conclusion he has already adopted; or to refute triumphantly in his eyes, any objections brought against what he is unwilling to doubt.

An argument which shall have made one convert, or even settled one really doubting mind, though it is not of course necessarily a sound argument, will have accomplished more than one which receives the unhesitating assent and loud applause of thousands who had already embraced, or were predisposed to embrace, the conclusion.

I am aware that there is in some minds an opposite tendency, to excessive doubt in cases where their wishes are strong;—a morbid distrust of evidence which they are especially anxious to find conclusive. Different temperaments (sometimes varying with the state of health of each individual) lead towards these contrary miscalculations. Each of us probably has a natural leaning to one or other (often to both, alternately) of these infirmities—the over-estimate or under-estimate of the reasons in favour of a conclusion we wish to find true. The difficulty is, not to fly from one extreme to the other, but to avoid both, and to give an unbiassed verdict according to the evidence; preserving the indifference of the *judgment*, even in cases where the *will* cannot, and indeed should not, be indifferent.

Obvious, however, as these principles must

appear, it is not at all uncommon to lose sight of them; it is not uncommon to hear wonder expressed at the supposed weakness of understanding of those who assent to arguments utterly invalid, but to which they have in fact never applied their minds. And it is much more common to hear some course of argument confidently proclaimed as triumphant and decisive in establishing or refuting some doctrine, merely on the ground of its being approved by those predisposed to assent to it. Whether, in fact, it be such or not, it is impossible *we* can fully estimate its weight till we have seen it tried in an even balance, or against a preponderating scale;—till we have seen how it is received by the indifferent, or the adverse. For through the operation of the principle I have been speaking of, arguments have commanded the unhesitating assent of all men, for centuries together, without possessing, in reality, any weight at all.

§. 3. It is, on many accounts, of great practical importance to trace, as far as we are able, each error to its real source. If, for instance, we supposed the doctrine of Transubstantiation to be really founded, as the Romanists pretend, and as, no doubt, many of them sincerely believe, on the words " this is my body," we might set this down as an instance in which the language of Scripture rashly interpreted has led to error. Doubtless there *are* such instances; but I can never believe that this is one of them; viz. that men really were *led* by the words in question to believe in Transubstantiation; for besides the intrinsic improbability of such an error having so arisen, we have the additional proof, that the passage was before the eyes of the whole Christian world for ten centuries before the doctrine was thought of. And again, if we suppose the doctrine to have, in fact, arisen from the misinterpretation of the text, we shall expect to remove the error by shewing reasons whereby the passage should be understood differently: a very reasonable expectation, where the doctrine has *sprung from the misinterpretation;* but quite otherwise, where, as in this case, the *misinterpretation has sprung from the doctrine.* When there was a leaning in men's minds towards the reception of the tenet, they of course looked for the best confirmation of it that Scripture would afford.

There is no instance, however, that better exemplifies the operation of this principle, than the one immediately before us—the Romish doctrines of the Universal Supremacy, and Infallibility, of their Church. If we inquire how the Romanists came so strangely to mistake the passages of Scripture to which they appeal, we shall be utterly bewildered in conjecture, unless we read backwards the lesson imprinted on *their* minds, and seek for the true cause in the natural predisposition to look out for, and implicitly trust, an infallible guide, and to find a refuge from doubts and dissensions, in the unquestioned and unlimited authority of the Church. This indeed *had* been gradually established, and vested in the Romish See, before it was distinctly claimed. Men did not submit to the authority, because they were convinced it was of divine origin and infallible; but, on the contrary, they were convinced of this, because they were disposed so to submit. The tendency to "teach for doctrines the commandments of men," and to acquiesce in such teaching, is not the effect, but the cause, of their being taken for the commandments of God.

Unwilling as men may be to submit their *actions* to an uncontrolled despotism, that indolence of mind which the Greek historian remarks as making them "averse to take trouble in the investigation of truth, and willing rather to acquiesce in what is ready-decided for them," has, in all ages, and on all subjects, disposed multitudes to save themselves this trouble, and escape at the same time the uneasiness of doubting, by an implicit submission to some revered authority. The disposition indeed to submit and assent implicitly, is (like all our other natural propensities) nothing intrinsically and essentially bad, when rightly directed, and duly controlled; but, like all the rest, is liable to misdirection and excess. Whatever is satisfactorily proved to come from God, is *entitled* to our submissive assent; and whatever there is of what He has revealed to us, that surpasses human comprehension, has a *claim* to be received on his authority alone, without vain attempts to explain or to prove it "a priori." That the implicit deference justly due to Divine authority, should have been often unduly extended to human, is what we might, from the infirmity of our nature, have even antecedently conjectured; and no one can suppose that this misdirected and excessive veneration originated in the Church of Rome, or is even confined to the case of religion, who recollects that the decisive appeal of the Pythagoreans to the "ipse dixit" of their master, was even proverbial among the ancients: and that at a later period, the authority of Aristotle on philosophical questions, was for many ages regarded as no less decisive. To question his decisions on these matters, was long considered as indicating no less presumptuous rashness, than to dispute those of the Church of Rome as to matters of faith.

§. 4. As for the local extent of the Roman Pontiff's jurisdiction, the claim of universal supremacy for *that particular See*, is of course an error of the Romanists as Romanists; for though the same encroaching and ambitious disposition may exist in others as in the Romish hierarchy, it must of course, wherever it exists, lead each to extend the dominion and exalt the power, of *his own* Church, State, Empire, or School, over others. But the tendency to claim or to pay undue deference to the authority of uninspired men, is an error of the Romanists not as Romanists, but as human Beings. The degree of respect generally paid and justly due to the authority[h] of the wise—the virtuous—the learned —the majority—which amounts to a *presumption*, more or less strong, of what they have maintained—a presumption which demands a careful examination of the reasons on both sides, before we decide against them—this respect was gradually heightened into a blind acquiescence, which forbad men even to seek for reasons at all. The morbid dread of uncertainty, perplexity, and dissension, led them to preclude all doubts as to the sense of Scripture, by a decisive authority; an authority which they pretend to rest on a text whose sense is in itself doubtful[i]; and thus to save, as it were, the ship from being tossed by winds and waves, by casting anchor on an object which was itself floating. But they succeeded in delivering

[h] An important ambiguity in the word authority will be presently noticed.

[i] See Blanco White's "Evidence against Catholicism."

themselves from actual doubt, though not from reasons for doubt; and were lulled into that apathetic tranquillity, which is the natural result of compulsory cessation of discussion. "Seeing then that these things *cannot be spoken against*, ye ought to be quiet," is an expression which may be used to characterize this indolent uninquiring acquiescence. They were to receive whatever the Holy Catholic Church decreed, or might decree, to be received; even though ignorant of what many of the doctrines were, to which they thus assented.

"Is it conceivable," they thought, "that the great body of the Church, including all its governors, for whose preservation in the right way so many thousands of pious Christians have been always daily offering up their prayers, and with whom Christ promised to be, always, even unto the end—is it conceivable, that all these should have been for ages together in gross and dangerous error on important points? No, surely," they said to themselves and to each other, "this is impossible; it could never have been permitted." Now if this is *not* possible, the Church must be infallible.

If we consider, in this point of view, the growth of the doctrine, we shall no longer think it so strange as at first sight it appears, that such a claim should have arisen. Nor (which is more important for our purpose) shall we think it incredible, that a similar course of reasoning should be likely to take place in the minds of Protestants, and should lead to a like result:—that the supposition, of any error in religious matters besetting wise, good, pious, learned, humble, and diligent men, should appear so *strange*, that at length the *strangeness* should be regarded as amounting to *impossibility*: and when once this point is reached, the claim to infallibility is virtually set up.

It must be admitted, moreover, that the claim of infallibility in the Church, when it is distinctly avowed, is at least more consistent—perhaps, I may say, more honest—than the sort of appeal which is sometimes made by Protestants to the authority of the " Universal Church," and which may be characterized by the homely though expressive proverbial metaphor, of "playing fast and loose." A person is loudly censured perhaps for taking a different view of some doctrine from that which, it is assumed, prevailed generally in the Church (i. e. the great mass of Christians) for many ages; the writers, termed "the Fathers," are appealed to; and it is represented as inconceivable, that the great Body of the Christian world should have long been in error on such and such a point. And, no doubt, there is a *presumption*[1] in favour of what has been long admitted by the majority; stronger arguments are called for against it, than if it were something novel, or the opinion only of a few. But when this presumption is adduced as nearly decisive, and it is then urged, on the other side, as it consistently may be, that the great majority, both in the Eastern and Western Churches, are, and have been for many centuries, and were, *at the very time referred to*, worshippers of relics, and of the Virgin, &c. the same Protestant advocate will reply, that these doctrines are *unscriptural*—that human divines are fallible, and that we ought to "obey God rather than man." Now if we regard the "Fathers" as men subject to human infirmity, and teaching truth mixed with error, we ought to appeal to them as such: if we appeal

[1] Elements of Rhetoric, part i. chap. iii. §. 2.

to them, or to any set of men, with an air of decisive triumph, we should be prepared to admit their infallibility throughout. It surely is not fair to make the Church's authority of the highest or the lowest value, according as it happens to support, or to oppose, our own conclusions.

§. 5. Indeed, monstrous as the Romish doctrine of the infallibility of the Church at first sight appears, and widely different as the claim is usually regarded from any that have ever been advanced by Protestants, there have not been wanting persons who (in consequence perhaps of the prevalence of the practice just noticed) have represented the Romish Church as differing little in this point from our own, and indeed every other. "It is true," (they say,) "the Church of England disclaims the right of requiring assent to any article of faith which may not be proved by Scripture: but then if she claims the right of deciding without appeal what doctrines *are* Scriptural, and requires of all her members the admission, not only of the authority of Scripture, but of her interpretation of it, and an admission of all the doctrines founded on that interpretation, the same end is gained: since even the Church of Rome *might* have professed to appeal to Scripture in behalf of all her doctrines, retaining the power of deciding definitively what books should be received as Scripture, and what is the true sense of each passage. "The difference then," they urge, (I am quoting the arguments of an author of no mean ability,) "between the two Churches, amounts only to this; that the one *cannot* err, and the other never *does;* the one is infallible, and the other always in the right." For though it is declared that *other* Churches *have* erred, and not denied that our own *may*, it is never admitted that ours (as constituted at the Reformation) *has* fallen into any error.

This change of advancing a virtual claim to infallibility, though specious at the first glance, melts away before a close examination; for, in fact, the claim of our Church is no other than even every *individual*, without any arrogance, advances, and cannot but advance, in his own behalf. Whoever professes to hold any doctrine, implies by that very expression his conviction of its truth. For an individual (and a Church no less) to acknowledge the erroneousness of his present tenets, would be a contradiction in terms. And the erroneousness of many of her *former* tenets, during our subjection to the Papal sway, our Church amply acknowledged by the very act of reforming.

But every Church must have certain terms of Communion, the rejection of which implies exclusion from that Communion; since the very idea of a religious Society is incompatible with a fundamental discrepancy of religious persuasion. And since such discrepancies may, and do, exist among those who agree in admitting the supreme authority of Scripture, it is plain that this admission cannot be of itself a sufficient bond of union. Our Church, therefore, (as every religious Society *must* do, either avowedly or virtually,) fixed on certain doctrines as necessary to be admitted by those who should be members of it; not denouncing as heretics[1] the members

---

[1] It is well worth remarking, that our Church has denounced the Romanists as *erroneous* indeed, but not as *heretical*. If one brought up in the bosom of our Church were to preach, for instance, the doctrine of the sacrifice

of other Churches who might hold different doctrines; but of course not admitting her own to be erroneous; which would be saying in the same breath that they are *not* her own. An individual indeed will often have *not made up his mind* as to this or that question; and will often express doubts as to some opinion which he is rather inclined to adopt: but for a Church to make a declaration of doubt, would be absurd. In whatever points our Reformers felt themselves undecided, and in whatever, though themselves convinced, they thought it unnecessary to require general assent—on such points they would of course say nothing. Whatever they set forth, they could not but set forth, as, in their judgment, both true, and essential.

It is possible, indeed, for a Church to multiply unnecessarily her articles of faith, and thus

---

of the Mass, he would be properly pronounced as heretical; but we claim no spiritual authority over the members of *other* Churches. The Romanists do; and accordingly denominate us, with perfect consistency, heretics; as being properly members, though rebellious members, of their Church. See Blanco White's Evidence against Catholicism, p. 118. and Hinds's History, vol. ii. p. 41—45.

narrow too much the terms of her communion: but if in any case this fault were committed, and even if we suppose many of the doctrines so laid down to be fundamentally erroneous, still this fault would be of a totally different kind from that of advancing a claim to infallibility [m].

In short, to *profess* certain doctrines, and

---

[m] Much of the confusion of thought which has arisen on this subject, is to be traced to the ambiguity of the word " authority;" which is sometimes used, in the primary sense, (corresponding with *auctoritas*,) to signify the weight assigned to the example or opinion of those who, in any point, are likely to be competent judges, and which raises a presumption in favour of what they have done or maintained; as when we appeal to the " authority" of some Historian or Philosopher: but sometimes again, and that not unfrequently, it is used (in the sense of *potestas*) to signify *power*, to which we are absolutely bound to submit; as when we speak of the authority of a Magistrate. The language of our Article keeps clear of this ambiguity, in the statement, that " the Church has *power* to ordain rites and ceremonies," (not at variance with God's Word,) " and has *authority* in controversies of faith." But still, the use of the word Authority in the sense of *power* is so common, that it has, I have no doubt, aided in producing the impression, that a claim is advanced by the Church of being an infallible interpreter of Scripture.

(which is implied by so doing) to declare that those doctrines are *true*, is, for every Church, allowable, because inevitable; to *err* in any of those doctrines, or in the mode of setting them forth, as long as there is a readiness to correct any thing that shall be proved at variance with Scripture or with reason, is nothing unpardonable, nor, in its results, incurable: while to deny the liability to error, and to claim, without warrant, the infallibility which implies inspiration, is in itself presumptuous impiety, and leads to interminable corruption.

For the difference is no mere theoretical nicety, but of most extensive practical importance. The claim to exemption from all error, *shuts the door against reform*. The smallest change in any article of *faith*, would break the talisman of infallibility, and the magic edifice of Papal dominion would crumble into ruins. In matters of *discipline*, indeed, the Romish Church might introduce reforms, without compromising her claim; since *there* the question is one not of truth, but of expediency; which may vary in each different age and country. But her regulations respecting discipline have been so intertwined with doctrinal points, that She has generally dreaded to alter any thing, lest her infallibility should be called in question. For instance, it has never been contended that the adoration of images and relics is *essential* to Christianity; there would therefore be no inconsistency on the part of the Romish Church in remedying that abuse: but it has been thought probably (and not without reason) that to do so might raise suspicions as to the wisdom of originally sanctioning the practice—as to the soundness of the arguments and decisions by which it was maintained against Protestants—and as to the truth of the miraculous legends connected with it; and the upholders of the Romish system have accordingly always dreaded (as was remarkably exemplified not long since in respect of some efforts towards such an amelioration, made in Germany) to touch a single stone of their infirm fabric, lest another, and another, should be displaced. For those who are conscious, or who at all suspect, (whether with or without good reason,) that great part of the system they are maintaining is thoroughly unsound, are naturally led to regard the beginning of reformation (even as Solomon says of the beginning of strife) as "like the letting out of water;" when once commenced they know not to what it may proceed, or how it can be stopped. And thus it is that the claim to infallibility burdens the Church of Rome with a load of long-accumulated errors and abuses, to which many probably of her adherents are by no means blind, but of which they know not how to relieve her.

To this evil must be added, that the claim of an infallibility independent of Scripture, naturally tends towards the result which in fact took place, the prohibition of translations, and the discouragement of the study of the Scriptures, as needless, and unsafe, for the mass of the Christian laity. And even after the removal or relaxation of this restriction, the people, even with the Bible in their hands, are evidently far less likely to perceive the erroneousness of any doctrines of their Church, if that Church does not profess to rest those doctrines on Scripture alone, but on her own independent and paramount authority. Thousands must have perceived many Romish tenets to be unwarranted by *Scripture*, who have yet never thought of regarding that as ground for calling them in question. On the other hand, " even corrupt Churches, provided they do not suppress the Scriptures, or disallow them as the only rule of faith, may still afford to many of their members the means of correcting their errors, and ascertaining the essential truths of Christianity [n]."

§. 6. But are Protestants then, as long as they do but acknowledge these principles, exempt from all danger of any such error as that for which the Romish Church has now been censured? By no means. Such might indeed have been the case, had the claim to infallibility for the decisions of the Church, and the comparative disregard of Scripture, been the *cause*, instead of being, as in truth it was, the *effect*, of the tendency to pay undue deference to human authority. The real cause of that tendency is to be sought in the principles of our common nature;—in the disposition to carry almost to idolatry the veneration due to the wise, and good, and great;—in the dislike of doubt and of troublesome investiga-

---

[n] Hawkins on Tradition, p. 42.

tion—the dread of perplexity and disagreement—and the desire of having difficult questions finally settled, and brought into the form of dogmas ready-prepared for acceptance in a mass. While this disposition ° continues to form a part of our nature, we can never, but by continual self-distrust, be safe from its effects. And the danger of virtually substituting human authority for divine, is the greater, from the necessity which exists of making use of human expositions of Scripture; not only for the purpose, above alluded to, of providing a Symbol, Test, or Creed, (such as our thirty-nine Articles,) in order to ascertain a sufficient agreement in members of the same religious Community, but also for the purposes of public worship, and of catechetical instruction. For the sacred writers have not only transmitted only one short form of prayer P, and no complete form for the administration of the Christian ordinances, but have not even left us any systematic

---

° Which cannot perhaps be so well described in our language, as by the words of the Greek historian, ἐπὶ τὰ ἕτοιμα μᾶλλον τρέπονται.

P Hinds's History of the Rise of Christianity, vol. ii. p. 114, 115.

course of instruction in the Christian doctrines. These, they have left to be collected from Histories and Epistles, evidently addressed to *Christians*— to persons who had already been regularly instructed (catechized as the word is in the original) in the principles of the faith : thus q, leaving, as it should seem, to the *Church* the office of systematically *teaching*, and to the *Scriptures*, that of *proving*, the Christian doctrines.

And it is a circumstance not a little remarkable, that they should all of them have thus abstained from committing to writing (what they must have been in the habit of employing orally) a Catechism or course of elementary instruction in Christianity, consisting of a regular series of unquestionable Canons of doctrine—Articles of faith duly explained and developed—in short, a compendium of the Christian religion ; which we may be sure (had such ever existed) would have been carefully transmitted to posterity. This, I say, must appear to every one, on a little reflexion, something remarkable ; but it strikes me as literally *miraculous*. I mean, that the procedure appears to me dictated by a wisdom more than

q See Hawkins's Dissertation on Tradition.

human; and that the Apostles and their immediate followers must have been *supernaturally withheld* from taking a course which would *naturally* appear to them the most expedient. Considering how very great must have been the total number of all the Elders and Catechists appointed, in various places, by the Apostles, and by those whom they commissioned, it seems hardly credible, that no one of these should have thought of doing what must have seemed so obvious, as to write, under the superintendence and correction of the Apostles, some such manual for the use of his hearers: as was in fact done, repeatedly, *in subsequent ages*, (i. e. after, as we hold, the age of *inspiration* was past,) in all the Churches where any activity existed. Thus much, at least, appears to me indubitable; that Impostors would have taken sedulous care (as Mahomet did) to set forth a complete course of instructions in their Faith; and that Enthusiasts would never have failed, *some* of them at least, to fall into the same plan; so that an omission which is, on all human principles, unaccountable, amounts to a moral demonstration of the divine origin of our religion. And this argument, we should observe, is not drawn from the supposed *wisdom* of such an appointment: it holds good equally, however little we may perceive the expediency of the course actually pursued; for that which cannot have come from *Man*, must have come from *God*. If the Apostles were neither enthusiasts nor impostors, they must have been inspired; whether we can understand, or not, the reasons of the procedure which the Holy Spirit dictated.

In this case, however, attentive consideration may explain to us these reasons. God's wisdom doubtless designed to guard us against a danger, which I think no human wisdom would have foreseen—the danger of indolently assenting to, and committing to memory, a " form of sound words;" which would in a short time have become no more than a form of words;—received with passive reverence, and scrupulously retained in the mind—leaving no room for doubt—furnishing no call for vigilant investigation—affording no stimulus to the attention, and making no vivid impression on the heart. It is only when the understanding is kept on the stretch by the diligent search—the watchful observation—the careful deduction—which the Christian Scriptures call forth, by their oblique, incidental, and irregular mode of conveying the knowledge of Christian doctrines—it is then only, that the Feelings, and the Moral portion of our nature, are kept so awake as to receive the requisite impression: and it is thus accordingly that Divine wisdom has provided for our wants, "*Curis* acuens mortalia corda."

It should be observed also, that a single systematic course of instruction, carrying with it divine authority, would have superseded the framing of any *others*—nay, would have made even the alteration of a single word of what would, on this supposition, have been *Scripture*[r], appear an impious presumption; and yet could not possibly have been well-adapted for all the varieties of station, sex, age, intellectual power, education, taste, and habits of thought. So that there would have been an almost inevitable danger, that such an authoritative list of credenda would have been regarded by a large proportion of Christians with a blind and unthinking reverence, which would have excited no influence on the character; they would have had

[r] Hinds's History of the Rise of Christianity, vol. ii. p. 236.

" a form of godliness; but denying the power thereof," the form itself would have remained with them only as the corpse of departed Religion.

§. 7. Such then being the care with which God's providence has guarded against leading us into this temptation, it behoves us to be careful that we lead not ourselves into temptation, nor yield to those which the natural propensities of the human heart present. For, through the operation of those principles which I have so earnestly, and perhaps too copiously, dwelt on, we are always under more or less temptation to exalt some human exposition of the faith to a practical equality with the Scriptures, by devoting to that our chief attention, and making to it our habitual appeal.

And why, it may be said, should we scruple to do this? giving to Scripture the precedence indeed in point of dignity, as the foundation on which the other is built, but regarding the superstructure as no less firm than the foundation on which it is fairly built? "I am fully convinced," a man may say, " that such and such an exposition conveys the genuine doctrines of the Scriptures: in which case it must be no less true than they; and may therefore, by those who receive it, be no less confidently appealed to. Supposing us fully to believe its truth, it answers to us the purpose of Scripture: since we can *but* fully believe *that*. For in mathematics, for instance, we are not more certain of the axioms and elementary propositions, than we are of those other propositions which are proved from them: nor is there any need to go back at every step to those first theorems which are the foundation of the whole."

The principle which I have here stated, as favourably as I am able, is one which, I believe, is often not distinctly stated, even inwardly in thought, by multitudes who feel and act conformably to it.

One obvious answer which might be given to such reasoning is, that to assign to the deductions of uninspired men the same perfect certainty as belongs to mathematical demonstrations, and to repose the same entire confidence in their expositions of Scripture, as in Scripture itself, is manifestly to confer on those men the attribute of infallibility. Believe indeed, we must, in the truth of our own opinions: nor need it be such a wavering and hesitating belief, as to leave us incessantly tormented by uneasy doubts: but if we censure the Romish Church for declaring herself not liable to error, we must, for very shame, confess our own liability to it, not in mere words, but in practice; by being ever ready to listen to argument—ever open to conviction;—by continually appealing and referring at every step "to the Law and to the Testimony"—by continually tracing up the stream of religious knowledge to the pure fountain-head—the living waters of the Scriptures.

There is no need, however, to dwell exclusively on the argument drawn from the possibility of our being mistaken; a danger which of course each one hopes, in each particular case, to have escaped. There is one decisive argument, perfectly simple, and accessible to every understanding, and especially acceptable to a pious mind, against employing any human statement of doctrines in place of Scripture, as the standard to be habitually appealed to: *it is not the will of God* that this should be done. For if it *had* been his design, that there should *be* any such regular

System of doctrine for habitual reference, and from which there should be, in ordinary practice, no appeal, He would surely have enjoined, or at least permitted, (and the permission would have been sufficient to insure the same result,) the framing of some such confession of Faith or Catechism, by his inspired servants themselves; since such a system would fully have answered the purpose in question, with the great additional advantage, that it must have commanded the assent of all who acknowledge the Christian Scriptures.

No Church, therefore, is empowered to do that, which God for wise reasons evidently designed should not be done. He has left to the Church the office of *preserving* [a] the Scriptures, and introducing them to the knowledge of her members, as the sole standard of faith—as not merely the first step and foundation of proof, like the elementary propositions of mathematics, but as the *only* source of proof; and He has left her also the office of *teaching* the Christian doctrines *from* the Scriptures. A Church is authorized to set forth for this purpose, 1. Catechisms—Homilies—in

[a] Hinds's History of the Rise of Christianity, vol. ii. p. 118.

short, whatever may be needful for systematic elementary *teaching*: it is authorized again, 2. to draw up Creeds as a test or *symbol* to preserve uniformity of faith in her members: and it is also, 3. authorized to frame Offices for Public-worship and administration of the Sacraments. But all these human compositions must be kept to their own proper uses. However wisely framed they may be—however confident, and justly confident, we may feel, of their truth and scriptural character—we must never put them in the place of Scripture, by making them the standard of habitual appeal. Works of Christian-instruction should be employed for *instruction;*—works of Devotion, for *devotion;*—Symbolical works, such as Creeds and Articles, for their proper purpose of furnishing a *test* of any person's fitness to be acknowledged a member, or a minister, of our Church. But never, if we would in deed and in spirit avoid the errors of Romanism—never should we appeal to Creeds, Liturgies, or Catechisms, for the *proof* of any doctrine, or the refutation of any error. Never must we admit as decisive such a syllogism as this: " the doctrines of our Church are Scriptural; this is a doctrine of our Church; therefore, &c.:" I mean, this must never be admitted, without immediately proceeding to the proof of the first premiss. And whenever we refer, in proof or disproof of any doctrine, to the Articles or Liturgy, for instance, we not only should not appeal to them *alone*, but we should also carefully point out that we refer to them not *as* the *authorized* formularies of a *Church*, but simply as the *writings of able and pious men*, which would be deserving of attention, supposing them to be merely private sermons, &c. To refer to them as *backed by the Church's sanction*, adds to them no legitimate force in respect of the abstract truth of any position. Such an appeal may indeed, in practice, be decisive, (and justly so,) as far as regards members of our Church: but it is, in truth, only an "argumentum ad hominem." If any charge is to be brought *personally* against an individual, as unfit to be a member or minister of the Church, the appeal is naturally, and rightly, made to her formularies composed for this very purpose: but when the question is not about a *person*, but a *doctrine*—when the abstract truth of any tenet is in question, " to the Law and to the Testimony!" It savours of the spirit of Romanism to refer for the proof or disproof of doctrines, solely, or chiefly, to any, the most justly venerated, human authority—to any thing but the inspired word of God. For if any one proves any thing from our Articles or Liturgy, for instance, either he could have proved it from Scripture, or he could not: if he could *not*, he is impeaching either the Scriptural character of the Church's doctrines, or his own knowledge of the Scriptural basis on which they rest: if he *could* have proved it from Scripture, *that* is the course he should have taken: not only because he would thus have proved his point both to those who receive our Articles, and also to those who dissent from them; but also, because it is thus, and thus only, we can preserve to Scripture its due dignity and proper office, and avoid the dangerous and encroaching precedent of substituting human authority for divine.

For it is important to remember, that human formularies, when once the habit is established of making a definitive appeal to them for the proof of any disputed point, have a tendency not only to rival, but to supersede, Scripture. They are usually drawn up in a more compact and regular form, such as to facilitate reference; and they are purposely and carefully framed, so as to exclude certain particular interpretations, which those of a different persuasion have introduced[t].

[t] It is on this ground, I believe, that the masters of several of our charity-schools are enjoined to confine themselves entirely to the printed questions drawn up for their use, and to give the children no explanations of their own. The consequence is, that neither master nor pupils are trained to exercise their minds in developing the sense of Scripture, but merely to exercise the memory in reciting words by rote. It is urged, that the master might fall into errors; and that though the framers of the printed questions and answers do not distinctly claim infallibility, their deliberate decisions are at least *less* liable to error than the views which might be taken by a number of comparatively unlearned men, and are less liable to be misunderstood than Scripture itself. The same reasoning would, if fairly followed up, lead to the substitution of Homilies drawn up by authority, for all other preaching; and, ultimately, to the confinement of the Scriptures themselves to a set of authorized interpreters. How easily one may be on the high road to Romanism without

The convenience thence resulting ought to put us the more on our guard against this encroaching

suspecting it! No doubt the Romanists are right in maintaining that Scripture is liable to be wrested by " the unlearned and unstable, to their own destruction;" and that it is possible to draw up forms so precise and systematic, as to be less liable to misinterpretation, and expressly guarded against particular errors which have been founded on particular misinterpretations of Scripture: and all this ended in their " taking away the key of knowledge, neither entering in themselves, nor suffering others to enter in." But even had they (which is inconceivable, considering what human nature is) embalmed no doctrinal errors in this system, they would still, as has been already remarked, have substituted a cold, lifeless, formal orthodoxy of profession, for active, vital, heartfelt religion. Our Church, accordingly, knowing that the attempt to exclude the possibility of error, leads to the suppression of practically-operating Scriptural truth, braved the risk of such errors as might from time to time arise, by suffering the people to study the Scriptures, and the ministers to expound them, according to the best of their judgment; not confining to the Homilies any except such pastors as might be judged incompetent to preach; and enjoining the Bishops to give all diligence in selecting learned and discreet persons for the Ministry.

And it would surely be the most consistent with these principles to select carefully the best qualified masters—to be

character of human compositions. More troublesome indeed may be the diligent search of the Scriptures than a compendious appeal to established formularies; but God has appointed that this labour shall be the Christian's lot, and shall bring with it amply its own reward. The care, and diligence, and patient thought, and watchful observation required in drawing for ourselves the Christian-truths from the pure spring-head, will be repaid by our having, through divine grace, those truths ultimately fixed in the heart as well as in the understanding;—we shall not only " read," but " mark, learn, and inwardly digest them," so that the heavenly nourishment will enter into our whole frame, and make us not merely sound theologians, but, what is much more, sincere Christians and good men, truly " wise unto salvation, through faith which is in Christ Jesus."

diligent in giving each of them individually the best instructions, and to superintend watchfully their instruction of their scholars, than to preclude them (as is in fact done, on the plan just alluded to) from giving them any instruction at all.

§. 8. It must not, however, be supposed, that those are exempt from the spirit of the error I am speaking of, who are the furthest removed from paying undue deference to the authorized *formularies of a Church.* Many such persons on the contrary are particularly addicted " jurare in verba magistri"—to adopt blindly, and maintain in defiance of argument, whatever they are taught by some favourite preacher, author, or party; whom they thus invest, virtually and practically, with infallibility. There is no benefit in an emancipation from the shackles of Rome to men who set up a Pope of their own making, or merely substitute an unerring Party, for an unerring Church; nor is any thing gained by abstaining from the use of the *term* infallibility, by those who believe in the *thing.*

Those among the clergy who are particularly zealous and sedulous, and particularly successful, in awakening sinners—in enlightening the ignorant—in administering consolation to the desponding, ought most especially to be on their guard, not only not to encourage but watchfully to repress in their hearers this error. " I depend entirely on Mr. such-a-one; he is my stay and my hope; I feel that I should be lost without him; I am sure every thing he says is right, and that I am quite safe under his guidance:"—this is the sort of language often heard, and this the kind of feeling evinced, in the case of many a one who has been recalled from irreligion, or rescued from despair, through the means of some spiritual guide: a deep-felt, and perhaps commendable, gratitude and veneration, degenerate into a kind of idolatry; and they at length come to exalt him into their mediator, intercessor, and divine oracle. This throws a most flattering temptation in his way; which he must be the more vigilant in opposing. He must not only be ever ready to adopt the apostle Paul's cautions, "Sirs, why do ye these things? we ourselves also are men of like passions with you:" "Every one of you saith, I am of Paul," &c. "Was Paul crucified for you? or were ye baptized into the name of Paul?"— but more than this, he must also warn his hearers, that whereas Paul, having been instructed by divine revelation, was an infallible guide, he himself, having no such inspiration, claims accordingly no infallibility; and he must therefore exhort often, and earnestly, the flock (not *his*, but Christ's) committed to his care; instead of pinning their faith to his bare word, to exercise their own minds—to weigh well the reasons he lays before them—and to study for themselves, as carefully as their circumstances will permit, the Scriptures which he is endeavouring to expound to them.

Still stronger to some minds is the temptation to become, each man a Pope to himself, by indulging the habit of making his decisions on some points like " the law of the Medes and Persians, which altereth not," and of enrolling them as it were in a certain code, which is thenceforward not to be open to discussion. Such persons make up their minds perhaps on few points, and with cautious deliberation; but having once adopted an opinion, will listen afterwards to no arguments against it. " I have long adopted" (says a respectable and amiable writer) " an expedient which I have found of singular service. I have a shelf in my study for tried authors; and one in my mind for tried principles and characters. When an author has stood a thorough examination, and will bear to be taken as a guide, I put him on a shelf. When I have fully made up my mind on a principle, I put it on the shelf. A hundred subtle objections may be brought against this principle; I may meet with some of them perhaps; but my principle is on the shelf. Generally I may be able to recall the reasons which weighed with me to put it there; but *if not*, I *am not to be sent out to sea again.* Time was when I saw through and detected all the subtleties that could be brought against it. *I have past evidence of having been fully convinced; and there on the shelf it shall lie.* When I have turned over a character on all sides, and seen it through and through in all situations, I put it on the shelf." The proceeding here described I believe to be adopted by not a few, though there are not probably many who would so frankly avow it. Yet such persons perhaps censure the Romanists for claiming infallibility for their Church; a claim not implying a pretension to *universal knowledge*, but to an exemption from the *possibility of mistake* as to the points we do pronounce upon; which points accordingly are no more to be discussed, nor any objections against them to have a hearing. Whoever therefore in this way decides on any point, does, so far, virtually, claim infallibility. Indeed if he did not—if he still admitted that he might possibly be mistaken on the point on which nevertheless he would bear no discussion, this, it is plain, would aggravate the fault.

"But," they say, "it is extravagant scepticism to be certain of nothing; it is an absurd and a wretched thing to have no faith in any thing, but to be for ever wavering and hesitating." I need hardly say that this is not what I recommend. The lover of truth need not be always in *actual doubt* on every point; but he must be always *open to conviction*—always ready to hear and to meet fairly, any seriously-urged objections. It is one thing to be without Faith, and another thing to have the Faith of the Apostolical Christian, who is "always ready to give to every one that asketh him, a *reason* of his hope." If there be any thing virtuous or manly in any faith, it must be in that which defies impugners—which courts investigation; not in that which rests on our resolution to shut our ears. If our confidence, for instance, in a friend's integrity is accompanied with a *determination* to hear no objections to his conduct, it surely is not so creditable to him, as if it rested on a defiance of accusations, and a readiness to hear all that could be said, though with a full *expectation* that all censure would be refuted. For we may very reasonably, on many occasions, feel, after a careful examination of some question, a confident expectation that no arguments *will* be adduced that will change our opinions; but this is very different from a resolution that none ever *shall*.

Yet nothing is more common than to hear a person say, in the course of some discussion, "Nothing shall ever convince me"....."Then hold your peace!" would be a fair reply, even before he had finished his sentence; " if you are not open to conviction, you are not qualified for discussion. The more confident you are, *on just grounds*, of being in the right, the more fearlessly ready should you be, to hear all that can be urged on the other side." I am aware that this is, in many cases, no more than a form of speech adopted from imitation: but considering how prone we are by nature to the fault in question, I cannot but think it important that even our language should be carefully guarded, so as never to express, what we should never allow ourselves to feel, that firm confidence in the authority of Man (whether the decision be another's or our own) in matters wherein he is liable to err, which is due only to the unerring God.

CHAPTER V.

PERSECUTION.

§. 1. THERE are several expressions of our Lord's which are calculated, and probably were designed, to guard against the notion, that a rejection of his religion is an offence which will be lightly regarded by the Most High;—that the gracious and merciful—the tender and condescending—character of the Gospel which proclaimed " peace, and good-will towards men," is to be considered as implying that men are left to accept the offer or not, according to their own tastes and fancies, and have no heavy judgments to dread in case of their not embracing it. On the contrary, " whosoever," said He, " shall not receive you, nor hear you, when ye depart thence, shake off the dust under your feet for a testimony against them; verily I say unto you, it shall be more tolerable for Sodom and Gomorrah, in the day of judgment, than for that city."

It was perhaps the more needful to guard against such a mistake as I have alluded to, on account of his having shortly before rebuked his disciples for proposing to call down fire from heaven on a Samaritan village which had refused to receive Him; saying, "Ye know not what manner of spirit ye are of; for the Son of man is not come to destroy men's lives, but to save." That this prohibition and this declaration of his, might possibly have been so interpreted by his disciples as to lead to the mistake in question, we may infer from the tone in which, even as it is, some Christian writers have spoken of the passage, as if designed to contrast the milder and gentler character of the Gospel, with the severity of the Mosaic Law. Whereas our Lord, in the words just cited, warns his hearers, and us, through them, that abundant in mercy as the Gospel offers of salvation are, that mercy is reserved for such as shall accept them; and that as the more glorious rewards, so also the more fearful judgments, of a Future Life, are held out in place of the *temporal* sanctions of the old dispensation. It is as if He had said, "Think not that because I came not to destroy the lives of the ungodly by temporal judgments, as Elias did, therefore the sin of these men is less, or the judgments reserved for them, if they persist in it, lighter; on the contrary, as greater miracles have been wrought among the men of this generation, and not temporal but eternal blessings offered them, so, a proportionate punishment in the next world, though they may escape in this, awaits the impenitent: I forbad you to call down fire from heaven on those who have rejected me; though Sodom would have repented if the mighty works had been done in it which have been done in these cities, and Sodom *was* destroyed by fire from heaven: verily I say unto you, it shall be more tolerable for Sodom *in the day of judgment*, than for them."

The natural inference from the two passages I have alluded to, compared with each other, and with several more in the New Testament connected with them, would plainly seem to be, that though the Lord will not, under the New any more than under the Old dispensation, permit his call to be disobeyed with impunity, the rewards and punishments which form the sanction of the Gospel are not (like those under the Law) temporal prosperity and affliction, but the far more important goods and evils of a future life; and that consequently the revelation of Christ cannot, consistently with its character, be either propagated or maintained by the sword or the fires of persecution, or by any *compulsory* means; but requires us to be " gentle unto all men, in meekness instructing them that oppose themselves, if God peradventure will give them repentance to the acknowledgment of the truth."

The desire, however, of saving men from the dreadful doom in the next world, denounced on those " who do not obey the truth," has often been a reason, and oftener perhaps a plea, for seeking to enforce a right faith, and to put down religious error, by all possible means. Too anxious, we cannot be, for the salvation of men's souls—for the diffusion and for the purity of the Christian religion—so long as we seek to compass these objects by the gentle force of persuasive argument and winning example: but when these methods fail, or even when it is apprehended that they *may* fail, the endeavour to prevent, by restraint, deviations from the established faith, and to force the stubborn and unpersuadable into that which appears to be both for their own good, and for that of the community, is perfectly natural and conformable to the character of man.

The Romish Church, which has so long and so loudly been stigmatized as a persecuting Church, is indeed deeply stained with this guilt, but cannot with any reason be reckoned the originating cause of it. The vast and black catalogue of her offences on this score, may be accounted for by the circumstance, that a large portion of *mankind* were for many ages members of that Church; and that in this, as well as in numerous other points formerly noticed, the evil propensities of man's nature were, instead of being checked on each occasion, connived at, sanctified, and successively embodied in that corrupt system. The pretended successor of Peter does indeed proclaim his own degeneracy, by his palpable disobedience to the command, to " put up his sword into its sheath;" but this, as well as the other Romish errors, has its root in the evil heart of the unrenewed man. Like the rest, it neither began with Romanism, nor can reasonably be expected to end with it.

In respect of the point now before us, this should seem to be more especially evident: for none complain more loudly of persecution than the Romanists themselves; who adore, to this day, the relics of the martyrs to Pagan persecution. And it is but too well known, that the Reformers, when they had detected and renounced the other Romish errors, had not, either in principle or in practice, divested themselves of this [a]. Even in respect of the persecutions directed against themselves, they seem to have joined issue rather on the question whether *they* were heretics, than whether heretics ought to be consigned to the secular arm. Nor can this remnant of the spirit of Romanism be so called, in the sense of making the peculiar system of that Church, properly, the *cause* of it; because we find the same principle manifested in its full force

---

[a] Jeremy Taylor advocated almost as a paradoxical novelty, the doctrine of toleration; and Locke found it necessary long after to make a formal and elaborate defence of it.

among the Mahometans, who cannot in any way be regarded as deriving it from Romanism.

It is derivable rather from the character of "the natural man;"—from the natural feelings, of resentment against opponents—of love of control—and of a desire to promote apparent good, and repress whatever seems fraught with mischief, by any means that present themselves as effectual. The bitter contests between the sects of the Nominalists and the Realists, in the age preceding the Reformation, present a memorable and instructive proof, that the operation of these feelings is not confined to the case of Religion.

§. 2. But natural as these feelings may be, and strongly as they may tend to produce persecution, it may be thought that, in the present age and country at least, it is useless to contemplate a danger now completely done away; since persecution neither exists, nor is likely to arise, among ourselves.

It is however important—not perhaps less important now than formerly—to lay down correct *principles* on this point, and to keep clear of a theoretical error, though it may not lead now to the same *kind* of practical evils with those which formerly sprung from it. For it usually happens, that a false principle will lead to two different evil results. To use a language which will be familiar to most of my readers, a false premiss, according as it is combined with this, or with that, true one, will lead to two different false conclusions. Thus, if the principle be admitted, that any *important* religious errors ought to be forcibly suppressed, this may lead either to persecution on the one side, or to latitudinarian *indifference* on the other. Some may be led to justify the suppression of heresies by the civil sword; and others, whose feelings revolt at such a procedure, and who see persecution reprobated and discountenanced by those around them, may be led by the same principle to regard religious errors as of little or no importance, and all religious persuasions as equally acceptable in the sight of God. To abstain, in short, in practice, from putting down heresies by secular force, if we at the same time maintain the *right* to do so, in the case of *pernicious* error, is in fact to sanction those heresies as harmless and insignificant.

Moreover, it is also important, with a view to future contingencies, to be in possession of just principles on such a subject. When persecution is not actually raging—when men's minds are not actually inflamed by the combination of religious animosity with excitements of a political character—then is the very time to provide ourselves with such firm-fixed and right principles, as may avail in time of need, and to destroy the roots of those theoretical errors which may lie torpid, yet ready to vegetate as soon as the season is favourable to them. For when party-spirit and all angry passions are raging, the voice of calm reason is not likely to be listened to. When the storm is in its fury, it may be too late to drop the anchor.

And especially persons of the mildest disposition, and most forbearing benevolence, who are fully, and perhaps justly, conscious, that they themselves would never, under any circumstances, be in danger of acting harshly—more especially, I say, should such persons be warned of the importance of tolerant *principles*, and cautioned to be on their guard against inculcating, or favouring, such doctrines as may, by being consistently followed up, lead others into persecution. For such a person is of course not likely to distrust himself on this point; from feeling confident that cruel severity is not his own besetting sin; and therefore may be in the more danger of promulgating principles, which others will act upon in a manner that would be revolting to himself. He may have been preparing a poisonous potion, which others will administer. The sword which he has unconsciously forged and sharpened, may be wielded with unsparing vigour by sterner hands.

And it should be remembered, that, however comparatively mild the character of the present age may be, if contrasted with those that are past, we still think it worth while to pray that we, God's "servants, may be hurt by no persecutions;" let us never therefore forget to add mentally a petition for the far more important blessing, that we may be preserved from hurting others by persecution.

To prove that persecution is unchristian, would be superfluous; since the proposition, so stated, would be at once admitted by all. No one calls himself, or probably thinks himself, a persecutor. The errors we are liable to on this point, if we *are* liable to any, must consist in our reckoning ourselves secure from this fault as long as we condemn the *name* of it, and reprobate the Romanists for being guilty of it, while at the same time we have a false or indistinct notion of what it is that constitutes the spirit of persecution.

I shall therefore chiefly confine myself to a brief notice of the mistakes as to this point which appear to be the most prevalent.

§. 3. I. The tenet of the Romanists, that salvation is absolutely impossible out of the pale of their own Church, has been not unfrequently considered as the necessary basis of all their persecution. But this view appears to me not only incorrect, but mischievous in its results. For though such a persuasion may be harsh and bigotted, and may tend to foster a persecuting principle, the two are by no means either identical or necessarily connected. It is at least conceivable that a man may believe a conformity to his own faith to be absolutely indispensable to salvation, and yet may hold, as part of that faith, the unlawfulness of employing coercion in its cause. On the other hand, a man may believe the *possibility* of the salvation of those of a different persuasion from his own, yet may think them much less *likely* to attain it; he may think their case not absolutely hopeless, but highly dangerous; and he may also think himself authorized, and therefore bound, to preserve or to reclaim men from error, by coercive means, when no others will suffice. He may consider governments as bound to exercise, in all respects, a *parental* care over their subjects [b]: now children

---

[b] Grotius, speaking of the establishment of the reformed Religion by the States of Holland, says, " Recepta publice disciplina quæ Genevæ, et in Palitinatu Germaniæ, passimque alibi, docebatur: hoc tamen interest, quod ejusdem religionis *alii*, diversas *minus tolerant:* Quippe, non in hoc tantum ordinatas a Deo Civitates ac Magistratus dictantes ut a Corporibus et Possessionibus injuriæ abessent, sed ut quo more. Ipse jussisset, eo, in commune coleretur; cujus officii negligentes, multos, pœnam aliorum impietati debitam, in se accercisse. Contra, istæ nationes," &c. The Dutch States regarded the maintaining of a false religion, as a *sin* only, not a *crime;* (according to the distinction so ably drawn by Bp. Warburton;) and consequently as not coming within the province of the civil magistrate: while others, misled probably, as men so often and so easily are, by the circumstance that in very many cases the *same* act will be *both* a sin and a crime, confounded

are withheld, and if need be, forcibly withheld, by their parents, not only from *inevitable* destruction, but from every thing *dangerous*, or in any respect

the two together; and regarding it the duty of the magistrate, as entrusted with the care of his subjects' *good*, generally, to enforce every thing conducive to what seemed to him their good, concluded that the toleration of religious-error would be as unjustifiable as the toleration of theft. Yet all this does not imply their conviction of the absolute *impossibility* of salvation to one infected with religious-error.

Some of my readers may perhaps imagine, that these notions, though prevalent two centuries and a half ago, have been long since obsolete among Protestants. But the following passages, breathing the same spirit, are extracted from a work which received the sanction of a large and influential body of Protestants within the present century. " Man is a compounded Being, not more impelled to seek his temporal advantage, than bound to pursue his eternal interests. Must not the State look to him in both conditions; and as far as possible assist its individual members in the attainment of both? Is not the Sovereign to rule for the greatest good of the whole? And can he leave out any part of that which constitutes their greatest good? Is he not again bound by the duty which he owes to God, so to govern his people as to enable them best to obey the will of the great common Sovereign of all? Must he not then secure for his subjects the best aids of Religion?" (On this principle I cannot conceive how the Sovereign can be justified in affording toleration

hurtful. The persuasion, therefore, of the absolute necessity of a right faith, however uncharitable it may be, does not necessarily lead to persecution; to any, that he thinks, religious errors, or in abstaining from suppressing them by the sword, if milder means fail; even as he would theft, or murder.) " In truth, every separation of divine and human things is a rejection of Providence." (The precept of " Render unto Cæsar the things that be Cæsar's, and unto God the things that be God's," seems rather at variance with this.) " I should not have dwelt so long upon so plain a proposition as that which affirms it to be the duty of the Sovereign to provide a *true* religion for his people," (this must imply, conformably with the foregoing principles, the prohibition of all *false* ones,) " but that, strange as it may appear, it is a maxim which hangs but loosely on the minds of many in the present day."

Whether the writer really meant to adopt the conclusion which inevitably follows from his principles, or whether he was merely designing to advocate what is commonly understood by " an established religion," I do not presume, nor is it important, to determine. Certainly the fallacy of proving too much, is one of those which are the most apt to slip in unperceived. It is remarkable, however, that he proceeds to censure, not merely the enemies of a religious establishment, but also some of " those who admit the lawfulness and necessity of an establishment;" including, particularly, Warburton; whom he describes as " feeling no concern for the truth of the religion which he calls to his aid," and as repre-

nor does the absence of that persuasion preclude persecution. And the notion is, as I have said, not only erroneous, but practically mischievous; because it naturally tends to make men regard with suspicion, as leaning to intolerance, every one who sets a high value on a right faith, regarding religious error as an important evil; and to suppose that liberality and christian charity con-

senting that there is "no difference between false and true religion in their influence on Society!" This is the inference drawn from Warburton's just and undeniable remark, that in discussing questions respecting the establishment of a religion by the civil magistrate, we must *waive the question* as to the *truth* of each, because each will of course regard *his own* as the true one, and there is no appeal to any authority on earth to decide between the different Sovereigns. Whether Warburton's views are correct or not, (which it is not my present object to inquire,) so gross a misrepresentation of him is neither fair nor wise.

But the writer from whom I have made these extracts might, consistently, (and this is the point which is important to my present view,) hold the *possibility of salvation* of one, whose religious persuasion differed from his own: how he could, consistently, admit of *toleration*, I cannot conceive. And what I am now occupied in pointing out is, the non-connexion of these two things, which are so often confounded.

sist in a carelessness about truth, and indifference as to all religious persuasions.

II. Another mistake as to the real character of persecution is that of regarding it as consisting in the employment of violent means *against the truth;*—as implying that the persecution must be on the wrong side. Those who take this view of the subject (as the Romanists seem always to have done) do not, in fact, censure *persecution*, as such, but rather *religious error*. They can no more be said to object to persecution, than a man could be called *an enemy to Laws* because he condemns what he thinks *inexpedient* laws, while he advocates such as he considers wiser. If the persecutors of whom they complain are doing only what *would* be right, supposing the doctrines they enforce were true, it is not properly the *violence* employed that is complained of, but the *false doctrines* supported by it. And it may be added, that, on this principle, the censure of persecution must be no less *practically vain*, than it is in itself incorrect; since no one will believe, or at least acknowledge, his own persuasion to be wrong, and the cause to which he is opposed to be that of truth. All dissuasives from persecution must pass by men " as the idle wind which they regard not," if the word be used in such a sense, that no one will, or conceivably *can*, apply these dissuasives to his own case.

III. Again, persecution is sometimes characterized as consisting in the *excessive severity*—the cruelty—of the punishments inflicted, and of the coercive means employed. But in cases where *any* secular punishment may allowably be inflicted, it can hardly be said that any can be excessive which is not as great an evil as that which it is designed to remedy, when no lighter penalty will suffice. Now the loss of men's immortal souls was, justly, regarded by the Romanists as a greater evil than the most cruel death of a heretic: and they were not perhaps mistaken in thinking, that such severity as effectually puts a stop to the offence, is, in the end, even the more humane procedure. On the other hand, where we have no right to inflict secular penalties at all, all alike, whether light or heavy, must be regarded as equally of the *nature* of persecution and cruelty, however unequal in amount. It is not the degree of suffering, but the just or wrongful infliction, that characterises each punishment. Persecution is not wrong because it is cruel; but it is cruel because it is wrong.

IV. Nor, again, is it correct to characterise persecution as consisting in the infliction of punishment for the gratification of *revenge* or *malice:* according to which view, two individuals might deserve, the one praise, and the other censure, while adopting the very same measures, the one from a benevolent wish to deter offenders, the other, from the impulse of angry passion, and from a bloodthirsty disposition. And it is certainly true that such an act as the prosecution of a robber, e. g. may spring from a sinful desire of revenge: but as in that case we do not condemn the act as in itself unjustifiable, though we censure the agent, so, those who hold the principle just mentioned, do not, in fact, disapprove of persecution at all, but only of revengeful *motives* for it. And any censure they may profess to bestow on persecution must be as ineffectual as it is in truth incorrect: for few will even think, and no one will admit, that he is actuated by revengeful motives. In the bloodiest periods of the Inquisition, the professed object was always the preservation of men's souls, by the prevention of heretical infection. Nor are such professions necessarily hypocritical. A man of the most humane and benevolent character may be led, by a mistaken sense of duty, arising from error of judgment, to sanction the most dreadful severities, which he regards as the only effectual check to a greater evil, such as he thinks himself bound to repress at all events. What candid (or even uncandid) student of history can believe Cranmer cruel and revengeful? Yet he sanctioned the cutting off of heretics by the secular arm, from a sincere, though erroneous, sense of duty.

V. Sometimes, again, the mistake is committed of characterising persecution as consisting in punishing men for their religious *opinions;* while punishment, for *propagating* their errors, is justified.

But this is in fact to explain away the very existence of persecution; since no man *can* be punished for opinions which he keeps secret within his own bosom. All persecution, if there be any such thing in existence, or even in imagination, *must* be either for *publishing* opinions supposed to be erroneous, or for refusing to *renounce* them, and to subscribe to the creed imposed. Will it be said then, that we are authorized to prohibit, and to prevent by penalties, the *preaching* of any doctrines we may deem erroneous, though it would involve the guilt of persecution to compel any one to abjure those doctrines, and to assent to ours? Surely this is drawing a distinction where there is no essential difference. If it is our right and our duty, to prevent by forcible means the spread of certain doctrines, and to maintain what we believe to be true religion, we must be authorized, and bound, to employ what will often appear the only effectual means towards our object, by compelling men to renounce those erroneous doctrines, and to profess that religion; or else, at least, to quit the country. For we should remember, that it never can, in any case, be left to our *choice*, whether we will employ coercive means or not. All punishment—all denunciation of punishment—in short, all compulsion and restraint—must be either a *duty*, or a *sin*. The Civil magistrate may say, "I have *power* to release thee, and *power* to condemn thee;" but he cannot have a *right* to do whichever he will.

And in the present instance, it is impossible to draw a line to any effectual purpose between forbidding a man to propagate his religion, and compelling him to abjure it, on the ground that the one does, and the other does not, offer violence to his conscience; which was perhaps the distinction set up by the Jewish Elders, when they were content merely to " charge the Apostles not to preach in the name of Jesus." Peter and John replied, that they could not but " declare what they had seen and heard ;" and it is not surely impossible, or even unlikely, that others also may think themselves bound in conscience to teach, at least, their families and their friends, what they conceive to be essential truths.

VI. Lastly, it is important to observe, that though persecution *itself* does necessarily imply the actual *infliction* of some penalty, we must by no means infer, that where nothing of the kind takes place, the *spirit* and *principle* of persecution is absent.

On the contrary, wherever this principle is

the most vigorously and effectually acted on, there will be the least actual persecution, because there will be the least occasion for it. For it should be remembered, that no one *wishes* to persecute. Penal laws against heretics, as those against robbers, or incendiaries, are not devised for the purpose of crowding the jails, and multiplying the number of criminals sentenced, but are designed to *prevent* the offences against which they are directed; and the laws are considered as then most effectual, when the terror of the penalties they denounce so operates in deterring offenders, that there is seldom any need to inflict the penalties themselves.

We never hear therefore of persecution in those countries where no resistance is made to religious coercion. The fetters gall those only who struggle against them. Accordingly, where the tyranny of the Inquisition reigns triumphant, there are no punishments for religious offences. No tree is withered by the frost of the polar regions, or by the scorching winds of the Arabian deserts; because none can exist in those regions. And no Protestant is now brought to the stake in Spain, because, there, persecution has done its work.

Hence the fallacious argument, for I cannot but regard it as such, which is often employed against persecution, on the ground that it does not answer its purpose of suppressing dissent. It is evident that *actual* persecution, when it does accomplish its object, must soon cease. The fire will go out of itself, when it has fairly consumed its fuel. The more effectually the Inquisition operates, the less it will have to do. There are accordingly few Roman-Catholic countries in which some attempts at reformation have not been suppressed by a vigorous, early, and steady resort to secular force; or in which such attempts are not *prevented* by the *apprehension* of it.

We must not therefore judge of the existence, or of the extent, of a persecuting spirit, in any case, by the amount of *sufferings* actually *undergone;* (else we shall suppose it to exist least where in reality it is in the greatest force;) but by the penalties *denounced*—in short, the degree of *coercion* that exists in religious matters. And in our own conduct, the rock of which we must steer clear, if we would preserve the true course of Christian meekness, is, not the actual practice of religious persecution, but the sanction of secular compulsion and restriction—not the actual *infliction*, but the *enactment* of secular penalties. For the *infliction* (in any case) of the punishment denounced, is an accidental circumstance; and it is never the object of the legislator's will, but depends in part on the persons suffering; and if the law is just, the penalty by which it is sanctioned *ought* to be inflicted on any transgressor of that law. And on the other hand, consequently, if the case be such that the infliction of the punishment *would* be persecution, the law ought not to be sanctioned by the denouncement of that punishment. A compulsory enactment necessarily implies the resort to forcible means, in case of resistance or disobedience; in any case therefore where the one would be wrong, the other cannot possibly be right[c].

[c] Accordingly, I have always been at a loss to understand how Christians, of those Sects which interpret literally the injunction to turn the cheek to the smiter, and which regard all employment of force as unlawful, can reconcile to their principles the practice (about which they have, I believe, no scruple) of *going to law* for the recovery of their rights.

If one of these has a sum awarded to him, whether in the

§. 4. The ultimate penalty accordingly, in this world, with which the Author of our Religion thought fit to sanction it, was (with the exception of a few cases of miraculous interference) the exclusion of the offender from the religious community which he had scandalized[d]: "if he refuse to hear the Church, let him be unto you as a heathen man and as a publican:" if he would not listen when repeatedly admonished, he was to be

shape of damages, or otherwise, he must be aware that the defendant would, in most instances, refuse to pay it, but that he is *compelled;* i. e. knows that if he refused payment, his goods would be forcibly seized by the officers of justice, and that an attempt to resist or evade such seizure would be punished by imprisonment or otherwise.

Do they then satisfy their conscience by the plea, that no force is *actually* used; the *apprehension* of it being sufficient? or do they plead, that at any rate the force would not be exercised by *themselves*, but by the officers, who are of a different persuasion? The former of these principles might be used to justify a man's sending an incendiary-letter, provided the *threat* proved successful; the latter plea might be urged in behalf of one who should hire an unscrupulous assassin to dispatch his enemy.

[d] For an able development of this principle, see Hinds's History of the Rise of Christianity, vol. i. p. 327—336.

removed from the Society. And it is worthy of being remarked, that the Romish Church itself claims no right to punish those who do *not* belong to that Society: a "*heathen* man" does not come under her jurisdiction. In order therefore to retain the right of coercion over all who have been baptized, even by such as She accounts heretics, the Romanists affect to regard them as truly members, though rebellious subjects, of the Catholic Church. In literal and direct opposition to our Lord's words, though censuring them for "refusing to hear the Church," they yet will *not* regard them in the light of "heathen men [e]."

The language of the Apostle Paul corresponds with his Master's: "a man that is an heretic, after the first and second admonition, reject." But no personal violence—no secular penalty whatever, is denounced against heretics and schismatics—"heathen men and publicans." The whole of the New Testament breathes a spirit of earnestness indeed in the cause of truth, and zeal against religious error; but of such a zeal as was to

---

[e] Blanco White's Evidence against Catholicism, p. 118.

manifest itself only in vehement and persevering persuasion.

This, which the Romanists cannot deny, they are driven to explain away, by saying, that the Apostles and other early Christians were *unable* to compel men to a conformity to the true faith; they abstained from the use of secular force, because (I cite the words of Augustine, a favourite authority with the Romanists) "that prophecy was not yet fulfilled, Be wise now therefore, O ye kings; be learned, ye that are judges of the earth; serve the Lord with fear." The rulers of the earth, he adds, were at that time opposed to the Gospel; and *therefore* it was that the secular arm was not called in against the Church's enemies.

But the Romanists might be asked in reply, if indeed such an argument be worth a reply, *why* the Apostles had not this power. Surely their Master could have bestowed it;—He unto whom "all power was given, in heaven and in earth:"—He who declared that the Father was ready to send him "more than twelve legions of angels;" whose force, as it would have destroyed all idea of resistance, would at once have established his religion, without any need of a resort to *actual* persecution. Or, if for any hidden reasons, the time was not yet come for conferring on his disciples that coercive power which was to be afterwards justifiably employed in his cause, we might expect that He would have given notice to them of the change of system which was to take place. But had He designed any such change, his declaration to Pilate would have been little else than an equivocation worthy of the school of the very Jesuits. Had He declared that " his kingdom was not of this world," meaning, that though such was the case, *then*, He meant it to be supported by secular force hereafter, and consequently to *become* a kingdom of this world;—and that his servants were not allowed to fight in his cause; with the mental reservation, that they were hereafter to do so;—He would have fully justified the suspicion which probably was entertained by many of the heathen magistrates, that the Christians and their Master did, notwithstanding their professions, secretly meditate the establishment of a kingdom supported by secular force; and that though they disavowed this principle, and abstained from all violent methods, this was only a mask assumed during the weakness of their infant power, which they would (according to the principle which Augustine avows) throw aside as soon as they should have obtained sufficient strength.

But the very idea is blasphemous, of attributing such a subterfuge to Him who " came into the world that He might bear witness of the truth." The immediate occasion indeed of our Lord's *making this declaration* to Pilate, was his desire to do away the expectation so strongly prevailing both among Jews and Gentiles, of a temporal Messiah about to establish a triumphant kingdom: but no occasion would have led Him to make the declaration, had it not been *true:* and it would *not* have been true, had He meant no more than that his kingdom was spiritual, in the sense of its having dominion over the souls of men, and holding out the glories and the judgments of the other world; for this was what the infidel Jews expected, and expect to this day; they look for a kingdom both of this world and also of the next;—for a Messiah who shall bestow on his followers not only worldly power and splendour, but also the spiritual blessings of a future state, besides. They did indeed expect the Messiah to reign over them for ever in bodily person: but the main part of their expectation would have been fulfilled, had He merely *founded* a temporal kingdom, and delegated (as the Lord did of old, to the Kings) his power, to his anointed, in whom his Spirit should dwell. Jesus accordingly not only *claimed spiritual* dominion, but *renounced* temporal: He declared not merely that his kingdom is of the *next* world, but that it is *not* of *this* world.

All the declarations, however—all the direct and indirect teaching—of Scripture, is unavailing to the uncandid inquirer, who seeks in these books, not a guide for his conduct, but a justification of it; and who is bent on making the word of God, where it does not suit his views, " of none effect, by the tradition" of a supposed infallible Church, or by the subtleties of strained interpretations[f]. But to a candid mind the

---

[f] " Quicquid recipitur, ad modum recipientis recipitur," is an ancient medical aphorism, capable of a wide application.

instructions afforded by the Evangelists and Apostles appear to me not only sufficient to settle all questions relating to the subject of persecution, but also (to the generality of mankind) better adapted for that purpose than any arguments which human reason could supply.

§. 5. For I am convinced, after much observation and reflection on the subject, that in all discussions, whether with professed Romanists, or with others, in spirit, Romanists, who advocate such principles as lead to persecution, the arguments drawn from Scripture are to be preferred for popular use, as best calculated to satisfy those who are of a Christian spirit, and open to conviction, but of moderate intellectual powers. Other arguments have often been unanswerably urged [g] against persecution, drawn from its ultimate inexpediency—from its liability to be employed against the truth, as well as for it. It has been condemned again with equally good reason—from its tendency to produce hypocrisy and covert atheism, and, by creating a general suspicion of

[g] Bishop Taylor and Locke have almost exhausted the arguments on this subject.

insincerity, to weaken the evidence in favour of a religion so supported. For the argument from authority—the confirmation any one's faith receives from the belief of others, is destroyed, when a *compulsory* profession leaves it doubtful in each case whether those others are sincere believers or not. And the prohibition, under secular penalties, of any arguments against a religion, does away with another and more important branch of evidence, *the defiance of contradiction;* through the medium of which most of the other evidences of Christianity present themselves to the minds of the generality; who could not possibly examine, in detail, for themselves, any great part (no one could, the whole) of the proofs of each of the historical facts on which our religion rests; but whose confidence rests, and justly rests, on the conviction, that if there were any flaw in the evidence, it would be detected and proclaimed[h]. Force accordingly,

[h] "Christians must generally, it would seem, believe in Christ, because their spiritual rulers do, and reject the infidel's views, because these people are pronounced accursed. Nay, the supposition of the clergy themselves having the qualification, and the opportunity to go through the process of proof, is only a supposition. They often want either or both, and it is im-

together with Fraud, the two great engines for the support of the Papal dominion, have almost anni-

possible that it should not be so. The labour of a life is scarcely sufficient to examine for one's self one branch alone of such evidence. For the greater part, few men, however learned, have satisfied themselves by going through the proof. They have admitted the main assertions, because proved by others.

"And is this conviction then reasonable? Is it more than the adoption of truth on the authority of another? It is. The principle on which all these assertions are received, is not that they have been made by this or that credible individual or body of persons, who have gone through the proof—this may have its weight with the critical and learned—but the main principle adopted by all, intelligible by all, and reasonable in itself, is, that these assertions are set forth, bearing on their face a *challenge of refutation.* The assertions are like witnesses placed in a box to be confronted. Scepticism, infidelity, and scoffing, form the very groundwork of our faith. As long as these are known to exist and to assail it, so long are we sure that any untenable assertion may and will be refuted. The benefit accruing to Christianity in this respect from the occasional success of those who have found flaws in the several parts of evidence is invaluable. We believe what is not disproved, most reasonably, because we know that there are those abroad who are doing their utmost to disprove it. We believe the witness, not because we know him and esteem him, but

hilated sincere belief in Christianity among the educated classes, throughout a great portion of Europe.

Such arguments, I say, as these, are sound indeed, and, to an enlarged and philosophical mind—one capable of taking a comprehensive view of human affairs and of human nature—they are perfectly convincing. And they afford to such a mind, a pleasing confirmation of the superhuman wisdom manifested in the Gospel scheme. For, men of that age and condition of life, and of the *Jewish* nation more especially, would never have been led by mere human sagacity to reject and prohibit all temporal coercion, and seek to propagate and maintain their religion by no force but that of gentle persuasion. And even in the present day, I cannot but think that such arguments as I have adverted to, are not likely to be comprehended in their full force, by men of narrow or uncultivated understanding. And there-

because he is confronted, cross-examined, suspected, and assailed by arts fair and unfair. It is not his authority, but the reasonableness of the case. It becomes conviction well grounded, and not assent to man's words." *London Review*, No. II. p. 361, 362.

fore it is, I conceive, that our great Master has graciously provided, in his holy Word, a support for the weak, and a guide for the dim-sighted, among his faithful followers;—that He has been pleased to reveal what is, not indeed undiscoverable by human reason, but yet not so discoverable as to be capable of being made clear to the mass of mankind;—that He has prohibited, both by the precepts and the example of Himself and his Apostles, that persecuting spirit whose inexpediency and whose intrinsic turpitude, some, even of the humble and sincere among his followers, might have failed to discover for themselves. As for the prejudiced and the wilful, they are not likely to learn the truth either from Scripture or from reason[h]: but the plainest Christian, who has indeed "the Spirit of Christ," and not that of the Papal Antichrist, may learn the will of his Master both by his teaching and from his pattern; and may be made "wise unto salvation," by becoming a follower of Him who was "meek and lowly in spirit,"—who "did no violence, neither was guile found in his mouth," and who "came not to destroy men's lives, but to save."

[h] "Remedia non agunt in cadaver."

§. 6. How blind even an intelligent man may be to the abstract arguments against persecution, is strikingly illustrated by a slip which the acute and powerful Bp. Warburton has made, in treating of toleration. He would have all men allowed liberty to worship God in their own way; but Atheists, he says, should be banished from every civil government, because they are " incapable of giving security for their behaviour in community; and their principles directly overthrow the very foundation on which it is built[1]." This great man overlooked the seemingly obvious circumstance, that, by a kind of perverse inconsistency, his remedy would operate precisely in those cases where his reason for it did not hold good, and would be almost sure to fail in the very cases it was designed to meet. Such Atheists as were, conformably to his supposition, utterly unprincipled and unscrupulous, would of course, were the system he recommends established, make no difficulty of denying their infidelity, and professing any thing whatever that might be proposed to them; those again, if there be any such, who were too honest to save them-

[1] Alliance between Church and State, b. iii.

selves from punishment by falsehood, would be the very persons to suffer the penalty. So that those to whom his description applies, as being such that the Community could have " no security" for their good behaviour, would remain in the Community; and the sentence of exile designed for them, would fall on those, exclusively, to whom the description did not apply.

A like error results, practically, in some instances, from our laws relative to oaths. I have seen a case recorded, of a tradesman suing a customer for a debt, which the other denied; he produced his books, and was about to make oath in the usual form, of the correctness of the entry; when the other party objected that he was an Atheist, and therefore was not entitled to take an oath: on being questioned, he admitted this; and the case was dismissed. The magistrates could not have acted otherwise, as the law stands; but surely the law should be altered when it operates, as in this instance, to defeat its own object[k]. The very purpose of

---

[k] See an able pamphlet entitled " Remarks on Oaths, &c." published by Hatchard, 1826.

an oath is to obtain some security of a man's speaking the truth: now in this case, if the tradesman had been so unscrupulous as to make a false charge, it is not likely he would have hesitated to support it by a false profession of his belief in religion. The best ground that could have been afforded for trusting to his veracity, was his refusing to utter a falsehood for the sake of establishing his claim; and it was for this very reason, in fact, that his claim was disallowed.

§. 7. The feeling which tends to foster the spirit of persecution, and to blind us to the reasons opposed to it—that feeling of *hostility* which naturally arises in our breasts against such as reject our Faith, or our own views of it—in short, against Infidels and Heretics—is chiefly remarkable from the circumstance of its being usually so much stronger, than our indignation against those who, professing our religion, disgrace it by an unchristian life, or even by an avowed disregard of religion. It should seem at the first glance, as if the very reverse of this were the more reasonably to be expected. For, as far as the *Cause itself* is concerned, he surely injures it more who brings discredit on it, than he who openly opposes it. The professing Christian implies, by a sinful life, either that his religion is compatible with immorality, or else that he professes it for form's sake only, and secretly disbelieves it; by which means he casts a doubt on the sincerity of the professions of others, and thus weakens the evidence their example would have afforded. And as far as the *individual* is concerned, the irreligious, or profligate, or worldly-minded Christian, is surely more chargeable with *impiety* than the unbeliever. An Atheist might, conceivably at least, have loved and obeyed his Saviour, if he could have been convinced of his divine mission: at any rate, he is not living in habitual defiance of a God whom he acknowledges. If two men receive each a letter from his father, and one of them, on very insufficient grounds, rejects it as a forgery, he is not surely *more* undutiful than the other, who, recognising it as a genuine letter from his father, puts it away carefully, and utterly disregards all the injunctions it contains.

The apostle Paul accordingly enjoins his converts to withdraw themselves, not from all intercourse with unbelievers, but from any man of their own Society, that " walketh disorderly;"— " if any one that is *called a brother*" bring a scandal on the Church by living in known sin, " with such an one not even to eat :" (i. e. at the Agapæ or love-feasts:) and to " cut off" (excommunicate) those who " offend" (i. e. scandalize) the Society.

How comes it, then, that men's feelings for the most part take an opposite direction? 1. One obvious cause, as far as we of the present day are concerned, is, that avowed infidelity is comparatively *rare*. We are so much accustomed, unhappily, to the case of Christians leading an unchristian life, while the open rejection of the Faith is an exception to the general rule, that in respect of the one, our feelings are blunted by familiarity, while the comparative unfrequency of the other fault, makes it the more shocking.

It is evident, that with the early Christians the case must have been reversed. Since men did not then profess Christianity as a matter of course, and had in general to encounter some hardships and inconveniences on account of their profession, an utter disregard of their religion, or a life utterly at variance with it, must have been much less common among the primitive Christians than among ourselves: while, on the other hand, they were living in the midst of unbelievers, and were themselves the exception to the general rule.

It is also evident, that the reason given does not apply, at least with equal force, to the case of persons holding a different form of Christianity. These are much more frequently met with than avowed anti-christians; and they are the objects accordingly, in general, of feelings less hostile than the others; yet still, in many instances, of greater hostility than is usually felt towards those who lead an unchristian life.

II. Another cause, which has the same tendency with the foregoing, is, that every one who rejects the whole, or any part, of our Faith, diminishes, so far, the confirmation which all men are disposed to derive, more or less, on every point, from authority—from feeling that others think with them. I suspect there are few, whose acquiescence even in the conclusions of Euclid, is entirely unmixed with this feeeling. In matters which admit of less intrinsic certainty, it is of course a larger ingredient in that compound of evidence on which belief rests[1]. And in proportion as each man is the worse qualified for reasoning, or the more averse to the trouble of it, he will be the more disposed to content himself with this description of evidence, and to acquiesce in what is generally received, without submitting to the toil of seeking for other reasons.

Now any one who rejects our tenets, goes so far towards shaking this confidence, and disturbing this indolent tranquillity; he drives us to take the trouble of thinking—of supporting our conclusions by argument—of contemplating and answering objections—and of making our opinions assume the attitude rather of frontier-towns, carefully fortified and watchfully garrisoned, than of secure and peaceful inland-districts. And hence we are naturally led to feel some indigna-

---

[1] In truth, as has been already observed, (in note *h*, §. 5. p. 252—254.) the existence of infidelity supplies one important branch of evidence.

tion against the causer of this disturbance. On the contrary, one who adheres to the belief of our religion, while it condemns his own life, is, in fact, bearing strong testimony in our favour, by admitting what, it should seem, he must wish to disbelieve.

III. Add to this, that one who is opposed to our Faith, however courteous his outward demeanour may be, and however liberal his real disposition, cannot, we feel, but inwardly look down upon us, as weak and credulous, or prejudiced and bigotted to error, or in some way opposed to right reason; and these sentiments we feel as personally *affronting* to us. On the other hand, he who, adhering to an orthodox Christian faith, lives a life at variance with it, seems to acknowledge his own inferiority to those whose conduct is such as, by his own shewing, his *ought* to be. The one in short seems to scorn, and the other to honour, us, not by their external demeanor, but by the very character of their respective opinions.

IV. Lastly, it will often really happen, and often again be supposed, and sometimes perhaps pretended, that a man's rejection of Christianity is, in fact, a *step beyond* his disobedience to it;—that he has *proceeded* from leading an irreligious life to the adoption of irreligious principles; and set himself against the Gospel because he found the Gospel against him. In this case it may be urged, with truth, that he is deserving of heavier censure than the Christian who leads an ill life, because he includes *both* characters. Whatever we may suspect however, I know not that we are authorized to impute these motives to any one without actual proof.

This last is, of course, the reason which, of all that have been mentioned, would be in general the most readily avowed, (and often in perfect sincerity,) to account for the greater indignation felt against Infidels and Heretics, than against irreligious or vicious Christians. I am convinced, however, that the other causes enumerated, operate not less powerfully towards the same result. And if such be indeed the natural feelings of the human heart, it behoves us to be ever on our guard against their excess, and against being led by them into those practical faults, to whose frequency history bears such ample testimony.

§. 8. That much of that kind of feeling does exist, which I have been endeavouring to account for, observation will, I think, sufficiently prove. And indeed it will often be found, that the very persons whose requisitions in respect of orthodoxy are the most rigid—who go to the greatest extreme in narrowing the pale of it—who make the least allowance for minute differences of opinion—and are the most bitter against all who do not agree with them; are the very same who go the greatest lengths of indulgence in respect of moral requisitions—shew the greatest extreme of tenderness towards those whose conduct is a scandal to Christianity—and seem as if they would have utterly disapproved the system of discipline, in respect of moral delinquents, which prevailed in the primitive Churches. I have seen accordingly severe censure bestowed on a sermon of a pious and able writer, in which he ventures to utter a wish, (far short, by the way, of that contained in our Church's Commination-service,) that those who are Christians only in name and profession—" who have no clear knowledge of what a Christian ought to be— would either take one side or the other; that they would either be the servants of Christ in earnest, or renounce Him openly, and say that they have nothing to do with Jesus of Nazareth, or his salvation. Happy indeed," he adds, " would it be for the Church of Christ, if all its false friends would declare themselves its enemies." The temerity of this wish, we have been told, would be such as to make us shudder, if it came from the lips of an enthusiast. No doubt more of the effect produced on some minds, depends on the question, *who* it is that says any thing, than on *what* it is that is said: for the framers of our Services have been so temerarious as to express an earnest wish, that the " godly discipline of the primitive Church" might be restored, under which those who had scandalized their brethren were put to open penance, or, as every one knows, in the event of their refusing to make submission, or of their not reforming their lives, were excluded from the Society, till they should so submit and give satisfactory assurance of their repentance.

We have been told, however, that in the event of even a voluntary secession on the part of " the false friends of Christ," there would be a vast portion of society permanently cut off from the ordinances and institutions of Christianity: (that is, I presume, as permanently as the unbelieving Jews and Gentiles, who might choose to make their own unbelief " permanent ;" or as the incestuous Corinthian, who was to be " permanently" cut off as long as he should persist in his sin and impenitence :) that they would cease to frequent the assemblies of the faithful—would never hear the word of doctrine or exhortation—would have shut themselves out from the appointed means of grace, and would be publicly and solemnly pledged to unbelief: that their hearts would be sealed against the voice of the Church, and they would be fixed to their life's end among the desperate adversaries of their Redeemer. The existing condition of things, it is admitted, is discouraging enough; but it is a state, it is contended, of millennial bliss, compared with what would follow, if Heaven were to listen to the wishes of this preacher: i. e. compared with the actual state of things in the times of the primitive Churches. It is urged, that now the unfaithful and double-minded Christian is perpetually and closely confronted with the principle he professes: the offices and ministrations of religion are loudly and incessantly appealing to the vows he has made, &c. &c.

All this may be very true; nor am I undertaking to prove, that the primitive Churches were not injudiciously strict in their discipline; or that our Reformers were not unwise for wishing its restoration; or that it was not a disadvantage to those Churches, that such as were strangers to Christian faith and practice, were not members of them as a matter of course, but remained avowed unbelievers till they were disposed deliberately and in earnest to embrace Christianity. The early Christians probably thought, that the ungodly or vicious were not the less, but the *more*, likely to be reclaimed, by the loud warning as to their dangerous state, which would be forced on their minds by their exclusion from the visible Church: that when not merely told from the pulpit, that the Sacraments and other means of grace are of no benefit to such as lead an unchristian life, but impressed with this truth by the actual refusal of these Ordinances, they would be the less liable to that common superstition of regarding these means of grace as a charm, and of flattering themselves that, if not in a safe state, they are at least in a *safer* state, by virtue of their going to church, and of being confessedly *Christians*, though they do not (as one may often hear people say) profess to be " Saints."

In all this however they may perhaps have been mistaken; and I am far from denying that there is much shew of reason in what may be urged on both sides. But what is to my present purpose to remark is, that those who are thus anxious to retain within the pale of the Church such professing Christians as lead a careless or immoral life, are not found, as some perhaps might have antecedently expected, to feel any thing like a proportionate tenderness towards differences of opinion. On the contrary, they are usually the foremost in exaggerating into fatal heresy the smallest shade of variation from their own views of orthodoxy; and the loudest in urging all those, openly and at once to separate from the Church, whose notions do not appear minutely to coincide with their own. If such arguments as those just alluded to were urged on behalf of those they denounce as heterodox—if any thing approaching to the same forbearance as they recommend in the case of immoral Christians, were proposed to be extended to such as have not quite made up their minds as to this or that doctrine, or have taken such a view of any points as appears incorrect in the eyes of others who lay claim to preeminent orthodoxy—were such a plea, I say, to be urged, almost in the very same words, I cannot but think we should hear a loud clamour against latitudinarian laxity and dangerous liberalism.

I am not of course contending that there may not be, either a defect, or an excess, of strictness, in the requisitions either of an orthodox faith, or of a blameless life: it requires a discreet judgment, to decide, in each particular case, under either class, the precise amount of the departure from the right road. But the circumstance to which I wish to call attention is, that since those who are the most lax on the one side, are the most rigid on the other, this confirms what has been above said of the tendency in our nature towards a more hostile feeling against such as oppose or disavow our religion, than against those who disobey and scandalize it.

And as this tendency is altogether *natural*, so it is, as might have been expected, eminently *Romish*. Never was there a more prevailing laxity of Christian morals, even among the very governors of the Church of Rome, and never was such corruption more lightly thought of by her zealots, than at the very periods when She was occupied in suppressing heresy with the most unrelenting rigour. Louis the Fourteenth, who, during nearly his whole life, was setting his subjects the example of living in open Adultery, was applauded to the skies by a Christian preacher, for his piety in having burned, gibbetted, racked, or driven into exile, hundreds of thousands of his Protestant subjects [m].

If we would be really safe from the danger of committing faults of a like character with those

---

[m] " Epanchons non cœurs sur la piété de Louis ; poussons jusqu'au ciel nos acclamations . . . . Vous avez exterminé les hérétiques ; c'est le digne ouvrage de votre règne ; c'en est le propre caractere." *Bossuet.*

which we regard with abhorrence in others, we must seek that safety in self-distrust—in a vigilant suspicion of the human heart.

§. 9. For it is to Human Nature we must trace, both this, and many other of those evils, which each man is usually disposed to attribute to the particular system he is opposed to. As the Protestant is often inclined to look no further than to *Romanism* for the origin of persecution, so is the Infidel, to regard *Christianity* as the chief cause of it. But both are mistaken. I am convinced that Atheists, should they ever become the predominant party, would persecute religion. For nearly the same causes, or others corresponding to them, would exist, which have been just mentioned as generating especial hostility towards those who differ in faith from ourselves. The Atheists would feel themselves to be regarded by the Christians, not indeed as weak and credulous, but as perverse and profane: their confidence again in their own persuasion would be as likely to be shaken by the Christian, as the Christian's, by them: all the human passions, in short, and all the views of political expediency, which have ever tempted the Christian to persecute, would have a corresponding operation with them. Not that I conceive most of them to have, themselves, any suspicion of this, or to be insincere in their professed abhorrence of persecution. As no one wishes to persecute, so they probably do not anticipate (under the above-mentioned supposition) such a state of things as would seem to call for coercive measures. They imagine, probably, that when they had deprived Christian ministers of endowments, had publicly proclaimed the falsity of the Christian faith, and had taken measures for promoting education and circulating books calculated to enlighten the people, the whole system of religious belief would, gradually but speedily, die away, and be regarded in the same light with tales of fairies. Such doubtless was the notion of some, whom I have known to express regret that Buonaparte did not employ the power he possessed in conferring so great a benefit on Society as he might have done, "by abolishing Christianity." They were thinking, probably, of no more active measures than the withholding of the support and countenance of government.

In such expectations, every one who believes in Christianity must feel confident that they would be deceived. At first indeed appearances probably would be such as to promise favourably to their views. For most of those who profess Christianity, merely for fashion's sake, or in compliance with the laws of their country, would soon fall away, and would be followed by many of such as wanted firmness to support ridicule, or the disfavour of those in power. But after a time, the progress of irreligion would be found to have come to a stand. When the plants "on the stony ground" had been all scorched up, those "on the good soil" would be found still flourishing. Sincere Christians would remain firm; and some probably would be roused to exert themselves even with increased zeal; and some apostates would be reclaimed. Complaints would then be raised, that Christian preachers decried, as profane and mischievous, the works put forth by authority; and that they represented the rulers as aliens from God, and men whose example should be shunned. Those indeed who had imbibed the true spirit of the Gospel, would not fail to inculcate, after the example of the

Apostles, the duty of submission even to unchristian magistrates ; but it is not unlikely that some would even take a contrary course, and would thus help to bring the imputation of sedition on Christian preaching universally. The rabble, again, would be likely occasionally to assail with tumultuous insult and outrage, the Christians ; who would in consequence be represented by their enemies as *occasioning* these tumults ; especially if, as is likely, some among them did not submit patiently to such usage, or even partly provoked it by indiscretion. And however free the generality of the Christians might be from any just suspicion of a design to resort to lawless violence in the cause of their religion, still it would be evident, that a revival and renewed diffusion of Christianity, such as they were furthering, must, after it should reach a certain point, endanger the continuance of power in the hands then wielding it ; and that such a change of rulers would put a stop to the plans which had been commenced for the amelioration of Society. Representing then, and regarding, Christianity as the great obstacle to improvement, as the fruitful source of civil dissensions, and as involving disaffection to the then-existing government, they would see a necessity for actively interfering, with a view (not indeed, like religious-persecutors, to the salvation of souls, but) to the secular welfare of their subjects, and the security and prosperity of the civil community. They would feel themselves accordingly (to say nothing of any angry passions that might intrude) bound in duty to prohibit the books, the preaching, and the assemblies of Christians. The Christians would then, in violation of the law, circulate Bibles clandestinely, and hold their assemblies in cellars and on sequestered heaths. Coercion would of course become necessary to repress these (as they would then be) illegal acts. And next .... but I need not proceed any further; for I find I have been giving almost an exact description of the state of things when the Christian Churches were spreading in the midst of Heathenism. And yet I have only been following up the conjectures, which no one (believing in Christianity) could fail to form, who was but tolerably acquainted with Human Nature. For " such transactions," says the great historian of Greece, " take place, and always will take place, (though varied in form, and in degree of violence, by circumstances,) as long as *Human Nature* remains the same [n]." Never can we be secured from the recurrence of the like, but by the implantation of some principle which is able to purify, to renovate, to convert that nature; in short, to " CREATE THE NEW MAN [o]." Christianity, often as its name has been blazoned on the banners of the persecutor—Christianity, truly understood, as represented in the writings of its Founders, and honestly applied, furnishes a preventive, the only *permanently* effectual preventive, of the spirit of persecution. For, as with fraudulent, so it is also with coercive, measures employed in matters pertaining to religion: we must not expect that the generality will be so far-sighted, as always to perceive their ultimate inexpediency in each particular case that may occur; they will be tempted to regard the peculiar circumstances of this or that emergency as constituting an exception to the general rule, and calling for a departure from the general principle. Whereas the plainest Christian, when he has once ascertained, as he easily may, if he *honestly* consult the Scriptures, what the will of God is, in this

[n] See Motto. [o] Eph. iv. 24.

point, will walk boldly forward in the path of his duty, though he may not see at every turn whither it is leading him; and with full faith in the divine wisdom, will be ready, in pious confidence, to leave events in the hands of Providence.

§. 10. I will conclude this chapter with a brief notice of some mistakes as to the real character of persecution, on the opposite side to those formerly mentioned. For as some may be in danger of unconsciously countenancing persecution by *narrowing* too much their notion of what it consists in, so others, on the contrary, by forming too *wide* a notion of it, may incur the opposite danger of comprehending under the head of persecution what does not properly deserve the title.

I. There is not *necessarily* any thing of the character of persecution in doing violence to a man's *conscience*. Though at the first glance this may be a startling paradox, it is evident on a moment's reflection, that to admit, at once, and universally, the plea of conscience, would lead to the subversion of the whole fabric of society. To say nothing of the *false* pleas which would doubtless be set up, when it was once understood that all were to be admitted, there would be no limit to the possible aberrations of even the sincerely-conscientious. Some sectarians have a conscientious scruple against paying tithes, on the ground that they disapprove of a hired Ministry. Not that according to the strict use of language the Pastors of our Church are *hired* at all; nor are the tithes *paid* by the farmer, since they only pass through his hands, allowance having been made for them in his rent; and he no more hires the minister than he does his landlord[p]. But still, as is well known, the collection of tithes has been complained of as persecution. On much better grounds might the same persons scruple to pay

[p] I have known a striking instance of the confusion of thought resulting from inaccuracy of language on this point. A farmer declared to a friend of mine, that he would not attend the ministry of *paid* preachers, but would listen to them only if they should go forth like the seventy disciples " without scrip or purse," &c. He did not recollect that in that case he *would* have to maintain the preachers, who are *now* supported by endowments. The disciples were directed, wherever they went, to " eat and drink such things as were set before them ; for the labourer is worthy of his *hire*."

taxes; (which they know are employed, among other purposes, for the keeping up of a *military* establishment;) since these really *are* paid, out of what was before (which the tenth sheaf never was) the payer's own property.

Some enthusiasts again, in the present day, have made it a religious duty to desert their wives and families, when these would not adopt their peculiar tenets [q]. Others, such as the ancient German Anabaptists, under the pretence that Christian men's goods are common, might incite their followers to a general plunder of those who had property, that the spoil might be thrown into a common stock. And some wild Millenarians, like the fifth-monarchy-men, might feel themselves bound in conscience to overthrow all governments, as the necessary preparation for the temporal reign of Christ on earth. In short, there is no saying at what point the plea of conscience, if once admitted without further question, would stop. The only possible principle on which we must draw the line, is, that the Civil Magistrate, to whom is committed the care of the temporal welfare of

[q] Fact.

the Community, should interfere in those cases (and in those only) in which the *persons or property* of the citizens are directly and confessedly concerned[r]. I say "directly," and "confessedly," because *remotely*, and *by inference*, every religious system may be made out to affect in some way the peace and well-being of the Community. There is, I believe, no religion existing, respecting which I have not seen an elaborate proof that it leads to mischievous consequences in practice, and that its professors are either likely to be, or, consistently with their principles, ought to be, the worse citizens; and again, I have seen the direct contrary inferred respecting every one of them. So that without the limitation above suggested, there would be an opening left for the forcible suppression, or for the forcible establishment, by the Civil Magistrate, of any religion whatever.

"But is the Civil Magistrate," it may be said, "to determine what are the cases, that call for his interference? And if so, how can any prin-

---

[r] "Render unto Cæsar the things that be Cæsar's, and unto God the things that be God's."

ciple be laid down that shall not leave him an opening to call in, whenever he is so disposed, the aid of the civil sword?" Certainly this is not possible. Coercive power *must* be entrusted to *somebody;* nor can those to whom it is entrusted be withheld from abusing it, if they are inclined to do, by any rule that can be laid down. It is notorious, that the Scriptures furnish none such; nor is it possible, from the nature of things, that they should. He who has the power, and the will, to do wrong, will never be at a loss for a plea to justify himself, even though he should be driven to maintain (like the wolf in the fable) that a stream flows upwards. But my object was, not to lay down a rule that should preclude (which is impossible) one who is seeking an evasion, from finding any; but to point out the principle which should govern the *conscience* of an upright magistrate: viz. to protect, by coercive measures if necessary, the peace, the lives, and the property of his subjects, and to abstain from all coercion in matters purely religious. But many persons are apt to conclude, that whatever is left to a man's *discretion*, is left to his *arbitrary caprice;* and that he who is responsible only to God, has no responsibility at all.

II. Although, however, such is, on Christian principles, the limitation of the Civil Magistrate's authority, there is no reason why the individual holding such an office should not also be a member, or an officer, of a Christian Church, provided he is careful not to blend together the characters of a political and a religious community. Coercive means cannot suitably be employed for the propagation or the maintenance of Christianity; but there is nothing that, necessarily, goes to secularize the kingdom which is " not of this world," or that necessarily implies the spirit of intolerance, in the possession, or in the exercise, of coercive power for other purposes, even by a Christian Pastor. Only there is the more call for care and discreet judgment in cases where the same individual has to exercise distinct functions, and especially if he is thus made to stand in two or more different relations to the same men. Such, for instance, is the case where the Rector of a parish is also a Justice of the Peace. Even if he were so not by an accidental appointment, but by virtue of some fixed general regulation, still he would be exercising, in respect of the same individuals, two distinct offices, regulated by different principles, and concerned with distinct kinds of subject-matter. In the same manner, if a military officer should chance to be also a magistrate, this would not imply his blending together the principles of martial law and of common and statute-law. So also some kings or other chief-magistrates hold also ecclesiastical supremacy; some bishops have a share in the secular legislature: others have principalities annexed to their Sees; and the Bishop of Rome in particular has long been a considerable temporal sovereign.

With respect to that Church, it is worth remarking, that the persecution and the other enormities with which it has been justly charged, have led many of those who have renounced it, to blend together confusedly in their thoughts every thing that in any way pertains to it. Whereas in truth, many parts of the Romish system, even such as are in themselves utterly indefensible, have no necessary connexion with each other, or with Rome. Her usurped Supremacy, for instance, and her false Doctrines, are two distinct faults; the latter of which is so far from being necessarily connected with the Church of Rome, that She scarcely differs at all in doctrine from the Greek Church.

And with respect to the point now before us, let it be supposed, (and the supposition, however unlikely to be realized, is perfectly conceivable,) that the Pope had, in respect of his *Diocese*, proceeded on Christian principles, and in respect of his *Principality*, had protected the civil rights of his subjects, leaving every one to exercise his own religion without molestation, as long as the temporal peace and security of the community remained undisturbed:—if, I say, he had always acted thus, as two distinct persons, it cannot be maintained, that this state of things would have introduced any thing approaching to a persecuting spirit—any thing savouring of that secular coercion which amounts to intolerance, and is at variance with the character of Christ's kingdom.

The question then respecting such a union, of civil office with spiritual or ecclesiastical office, in the same individual, becomes one of mere expediency; and one which of course will vary in its complexion, according to the circumstances of each country or period. What we are at present concerned with is, merely to determine what does or does not involve the principle of persecution; i. e. the employment or the denouncement of coercion in matters of religion.

III. There is nothing, *necessarily*, of the spirit of persecution in a man's requiring his servants, or his tenants, or the tradesmen he deals with, or all that associate with him, to be pious characters, or to be of his own religious persuasion or practice, even down to the minutest particulars [r]. This is so evident, that it would not have needed being mentioned, but that we are so liable to have our thoughts insensibly led astray by language [s]. We hear, for instance, of a man's being *compelled* to adopt this or that form of religion, as a condition of being in such-a-one's service, or of obtaining a renewal of a lease; and we are thence liable to forget, what is plain as soon as we reflect on it, that this is not *absolute* compulsion, since it interferes with no man's *natural*,

---

[r] I mean, of course, supposing him not to disappoint any *expectations* that may reasonably have been formed; for reasonable expectation is a ground of *equitable right*.

[s] Elements of Logic, chap. iii. §. 5.

or *previously existing, rights* [t]; and that to prohibit such a procedure *would* be an interference with the right of the other " to do what he will with his own." Such a mode of conduct, as I have been alluding to, might indeed be carried to such a length, as justly to incur the censure of indiscretion—of bigotry—of illiberality; it might be such as even to indicate in the individual a disposition [u] which would lead him to persecute if he had the power; but still it would not in itself involve the principle of persecution.

The same reasoning will apply to the case of the exclusion from certain endowments of one not belonging to the Church for whose benefit they

---

[t] I cannot but think, however, that there is ground of complaint when a man cannot obtain his rights, whether those to which all men are entitled by nature, or those of the citizens of his particular community, without either taking some oath, or going through some other religious ceremony, against which he has a conscientious scruple. A special indulgence has been granted to the Quakers in respect of oaths and the marriage-service; but if this was reasonable in principle, I cannot see why the principle should not have been recognized, and acted upon uniformly.

[u] See above, §. 3. subsect. I. of this chapter.

are designed. A man is said to be *compelled* to subscribe the Thirty-nine Articles, if he would hold a Church-living, or a Fellowship: he is compelled to be a Presbyterian, if he would hold the office of Minister at a Presbyterian chapel, &c. So also in order to obtain a Degree, he *must* have kept certain academical terms, and must undergo an examination in certain prescribed branches of learning; nay, in order to hold a Scholarship on some particular foundations, he *must* be a native of a certain district; and if he would retain his situation, he must remain unmarried. It is evident, on a moment's reflection, that though we use in such cases the *words* "must," "obliged," "forced," &c. all this has nothing to do with absolute coercion [x].

On the same principle it may be maintained, that there is nothing, necessarily, of the character of intolerance, in precluding those who are not members of a particular Church from having any share in legislating for that Church, in respect of matters of a purely spiritual or ecclesiastical character: indeed to admit them to such

---

[x] See Appendix to Elements of Logic; article "Necessary."

a share, is a manifest anomaly and inconsistency, though one which may sometimes be in practice unavoidable or insignificant. That none but Quakers, for instance, or Methodists, have a voice in the general Assemblies of Quakers, or of Methodists, respectively, is so far from being at all to be complained of as savouring of an intolerant spirit, that, on the contrary, as long as they confine themselves to matters exclusively religious, they would justly regard the interference of those not belonging to their sect, as a violation of the principle of toleration. And the *anomaly* is in itself just as *real*, whether in practice it lead to the most *important* or the most *trifling* results;—whether, for instance, a majority of the Assembly which governs a particular Church, be of a different persuasion, or whether *one single* Roman-Catholic or Dissenter have a voice in the election of a member of that Assembly ^y.

^y Some are apt to express themselves as if the anomaly consisted merely in members of the *Church of Rome* legislating for a Protestant Church. Suppose that some particular description of Protestants, or, if you will, that all Protestants, are more pure in their faith—less dangerous in their principles

But then, it may be said, if it so happen (as is the case among us in practice, though not by original appointment, according to the theory of the constitution, and early usage [z]) that the As-

—less hostile to our Church—than the Romanists; still the question remains the same, what has any man to do with the regulations of a Church he does not belong to?

But some persons are even accustomed to speak of " the Protestant religion," and even of " the Protestant Church," without reflecting whether there are any such things, or whether they are employing words without any distinct meaning.

Dr. Hawkins, I am happy to find, has forestalled me in part of this remark. " The term ' Protestant,' when it denotes a member of one of the Western Churches who is free from Romish error, is merely a term of convenience. It may be employed perhaps with little regard to history or etymology; but it answers its intended purpose, and it does no harm. Not so, such a phrase as ' the Protestant religion.' The very expression, whenever it is not evidently synonymous with ' the religion of the Protestant Church of England,' implies inattention to the fact, that there is no one religion common to Protestants as contradistinguished from the Romanists; and it tends to throw a veil over another important fact, that the creeds of certain Protestant sects are far more remote than that of the Church of Rome from the truth of the Gospel." *Sermon preached at Maldon*, p. 6.

[z] See Field's work on Church Government.

sembly, which alone exercises the right of legislating for the Church, in all matters, is also the supreme legislating-body in secular concerns; does it not savour of intolerance to exclude, by a test-law, from such an Assembly, or from voting for those who are to sit in it, men otherwise qualified? Granted that they have nothing to do with the internal regulations of a Church to which they do not belong; the same cannot be said of the taxes imposed, and the laws enacted, by that same Assembly. In despotic countries, indeed, the people have nothing to do with the taxes, but to pay them, or with the laws, but to submit to them: but in a free country, it cannot be maintained, that to preclude from all share in legislating, or in appointing legislators, in secular matters, one who is not disqualified in respect of *that particular branch* of business, does not deprive him of any of his rights, or that it is not as great an anomaly as to *admit* him to interfere in Church matters in respect of which he *is* disqualified.

Such are, in the abstract, the conflicting difficulties in the case. It is as if a man should put in an equitable claim to a house, some parts of which are confessedly none of his; or to a piece of land, on which there are buildings erected, to which he has no right. The problem, to keep clear of both of these opposite anomalies, has not, I think, yet been solved[a]; nor has it, I think, hitherto been generally contemplated with sufficient clearness and steadiness to allow of a fair trial, whether it can be solved or not: though about thirty years ago steps began to be taken

---

[a] It ought to be mentioned, in justice to Mr. Wilmot Horton, that he is one of the few persons who have seen and fairly met the difficulty. I cannot but think indeed, that, according to his scheme, (see " Protestant Securities,") other difficulties would have arisen, in the practical adjustment of the questions as to each measure, whether it concerned the Church *only*, or affected also the *property and civil rights* of the Community. Still, he seems to have fixed on the right *principle;* which might, I should think, by some contrivance or other, have been adapted to practice. At least the main objection usually alleged against his proposal, that it would constitute in fact *two* legislative assemblies for two distinct branches of legislation, has always appeared to me its chief recommendation. The distribution of the several offices among the several Ministers of State, viz. Chancellor of the Exchequer, Secretary for the Home Department—for Foreign Affairs, &c. is open to the same objection.

with a view to the practical adjustment of the difficulties. My object in touching upon the question at present is no more than, (confining myself to the proper topics of this work,) to point out in what relation that question stands to the subject of the present chapter [b].

IV. Lastly, there is nothing, necessarily, of intolerance, in protecting, by coercive means if needful, the professors of any religion, against violence or plunder, disturbance to their religious meetings, insult, libel, or any other such molestation, from those of an adverse party.

[b] I have alluded merely to the grant to Roman-Catholics of the *elective franchise*, and to the suspension of the *operation* of the test-law for excluding Dissenters, because in these consisted the *anomaly*, which alone it is for my present purpose to treat of. As for the greater or less *political* danger of any of the measures subsequently proposed or adopted, it would be foreign to the purpose of the present work to enter on the discussion of these, or any other, political questions. Whether it were a safer course to leave the test-law dormant, or formally to repeal it—to confine the Roman-Catholic electors to the choice of a Protestant representative, or to leave them at liberty to elect one of their own persuasion—these, and all such questions of political expediency, I pass by as not properly connected with the matter in hand.

Such protection is so far from being at variance with the principles above laid down, that it is an application of them. It is not persecution, but the prevention of persecution. For *lawless and irregular* outrage is not, for that reason, the less of the character of persecution; and the unauthorized cruelties of the people were, we may be sure, among the severest trials the early Christians had to undergo. And yet there are some persons who are ready to denounce as persecuting, every system which does not leave them at liberty to persecute others.

It must not be forgotten, however, that when the religion, in behalf of which the Civil Magistrate has been driven to interfere, happens to be *his own*, he will be strongly tempted not to stop short at measures of mere immediate self-defence, but to take what will seem the effectual step, of putting down altogether the hostile party.

To guard against overstepping the proper line of procedure in this matter, and also to decide on what occasions the appeal to the interference of the Civil power is not only justifiable, but expedient also, are points which must, in each particular instance, be left to the head and the heart of each individual. General principles may be sketched out; but there can be none that will teach their own application, or supersede the exercise of practical good sense, cautious deliberation, and Christian candour.

It may be worth while, however, to observe, in conclusion, how important it is always to keep in mind, that the CROSS which our Master and his Apostles bore so meekly, our proud nature strongly impels us to refuse, whenever we can, by any means whatsoever, avoid it. We are tempted, to admire at a distance, while we revolt at the thought of copying, their patience under calumny and derision, and every kind of provocation. And, what is more, this pride of the human heart is apt to disguise itself to our conscience under the appearance of piety; we are in danger, I mean, of regarding as zeal for God's honour, what is perhaps, in truth, rather, zeal for our own honour. He who does but reject our faith, implies, as I have observed above, something affronting to ourselves; much more, if he slander and insult us for maintaining it: and it is from this cause that we are prone to feel greater indignation at such conduct, than at the equal affront offered to God by those who acknowledge his claim, while in their lives they habitually disregard it, to their love, gratitude, veneration, and obedience. But yet, as every one who insults us on account of our religion, does by so doing insult that religion itself, we are likely to flatter ourselves that this last is the sole ground of our indignation; when in fact, perhaps, our personal feelings have a great share in it.

But we must not expect, till the Church militant is exchanged for the Church triumphant, that Christ's devoted followers will have no Cross to bear, or that they will encounter no opposition or molestation from his enemies. At least, till the World, even what is called the Christian World, shall have become much more imbued with the spirit of Christianity than it ever has been yet, our Lord's warnings to his disciples must be regarded as in some degree applicable to us: " If the World hate you, ye know that it hated Me before it hated you . . . because ye are not of the World, therefore the World hateth you." The Christian who is steady and unshrinking, and active in his Master's cause, though it is his duty not wantonly to provoke obloquy and opposition, by any indiscreet or violent conduct, yet must not expect always to escape such mortifications; and he should be prepared so to meet them, as to shew how far beyond " the praise of men" he prizes the approbation of Him " who seeth in secret."

Still, cases may undoubtedly occur, in which it will be our right and our duty to use means for protecting ourselves or others, against lawless aggression. No rule, as I have said, can be laid down, which will supersede the exercise of a sound and unbiassed judgment, for deciding in each particular instance whether it is allowable and advisable to call in the aid of the secular arm for the protection of the professors of religion. The right medium, says the great Master of ancient moralists, must be fixed in each particular instance by each man's discretion: but he proceeds to give the best general caution that can be supplied; viz. to lean always towards the safer side; ever avoiding the more sedulously the worse extreme, and regarding that as the worse, to which we are by *nature the more prone*[c]

[c] Arist. Eth. b. ii. ch. 9.

On this principle we should always, in respect of any matters connected with our religion, be more willing to have it asked, *why we do not*, than why we *do*, resort to the aid of the Civil power.

And even when we have fully determined what procedure is *in itself* right, we must be still watchful over our own heart, subjecting our *motives* to the severest scrutiny, and taking care that we do not inwardly applaud and sanctify in our own eyes, as a virtuous jealousy for God's glory, what may be in reality chiefly a regard for our own credit, and a tenderness for our own ease and comfort.

CHAPTER VI.

TRUST IN NAMES AND PRIVILEGES.

§. 1. MANKIND have a natural tendency to pride themselves on the advantages they enjoy—on the privileges they possess—on the titles they bear as badges of those privileges—and especially on their being members of any Society or class endowed with such privileges. And they are disposed not only to feel a pride and satisfaction in possessing such advantages, but also carelessly to put their trust in these, independently of the use made of them, as necessarily implying some superior benefit to the possessor.

How strongly this tendency operated among the Jews of old, we have ample proof in the Bible. Even under the Old dispensation we may gather from the writings of the prophets, that, in spite of their numberless backslidings, they still flattered themselves that, as the Lord's chosen and peculiar people, and as having among them the only Temple of the true God, He would not execute on them the judgments He had denounced. And when their captivity and the destruction of their temple had undeceived them in this point, they still clung to the hope of the promised Messiah to arise from among them, and who should "restore all things." In this hope, indeed, they were not erroneous; but their error was, in trusting that they should surely be partakers of the promised benefits, by virtue of their privilege as Abraham's children, of the stock of his chosen descendant Judah, whatever might be their own conduct; and that no such change of dispensation could take place as should put even the least deserving Jew below, or even on a level with, the best of the unclean and despised race of the Gentiles.

Accordingly, John the Baptist takes occasion to warn them on this head at the opening of his ministry; "Now is the axe laid to the root of the tree: every tree therefore that bringeth not forth good fruit, is hewn down, and cast into the fire. And think not to say within yourselves, we have Abraham to our father; for I say unto you, that God is able of these stones to raise up children unto Abraham." The Apostle Paul in like manner is compelled incessantly to warn the Jewish believers, that " there is no difference" between the Jewish and the Greek Christian, inasmuch as " all have sinned and come short of the glory of God;"—that there is " neither Jew nor Greek—neither Barbarian, Scythian, bond, or free;" and that " in Christ Jesus neither circumcision nor uncircumcision profiteth any thing, but a new creature;" and that the believing Gentiles are adopted as equally God's children, and heirs of his promises, no less than the natural descendants of Abraham.

Nor is he merely warning Christians that God is " no respecter of persons," (as it had been first revealed to Peter,) and that " in every nation he that feareth Him, and worketh righteousness, is accepted of Him"—not only are the *workers of righteousness* cautioned against supposing that the Jews by nature, or the adherents to the ceremonial Law, were to obtain a higher share of divine favour; but, what may seem more strange, the Apostle finds it necessary to guard them against the error of trusting in the circumstance of being *under* the Law, independently of the *observance* of it; as if a certain degree, at least, of divine favour was secured by the mere circumstance of having received by Revelation the divine commands, even though they were not careful to obey them. The greater part of the early portion of the Epistle to the Romans is taken up in combating this strange delusion: he assures them, that " not the *hearers* of the Law are just before God, but the doers of the Law shall be justified:" " behold," says he, " thou art called a Jew, and restest in the Law, and makest thy boast of God;" and yet these same persons he speaks of as dishonouring God, by breaking the Law in which they made their boast, so notoriously, that the name of God was " blasphemed among the Gentiles through them."

§. 2. A like error seems to have prevailed no less among the early Christians generally, in respect of the pride and vain-confidence with which *they* regarded their privileges as Christians. The Apostle warns them in the same Epistle, that as the natural branch (i. e. the Israelites after the flesh) had been broken off, and they grafted in, so, a like severity was to be expected by them also, as God had exercised towards the disobedient among his favoured people of old, if, instead of making the best use of his mercies, they were high-minded—puffed up, i. e. with boastful confidence in their peculiar privileges, and neglectful of the peculiar responsibility these imposed. "If God," he admonishes them, "spared not the natural branches, take heed lest He also spare not thee." And in the same tone he warns the Corinthians not to rely in security on their being God's elect people, from the example of the Israelites, who were also, all of them, "God's elect[a]," yet of whom one whole generation were cut off, by various judgments, in the wilderness, for their disobedience: the history of these things, he says, was "written for our admonition; wherefore let him that thinketh he standeth take heed lest he fall." And the Apostle Jude again seems to apprehend the same danger for those he is addressing, and cautions them by the same example, "how the Lord *after having saved the people* out of the land of Egypt, afterwards destroyed them that believed not."

[a] Essay iii. Second Series.

And as, in the first ages of Christianity, Christians were likely to feel this proud confidence in *that* title, as distinguished from unbelieving Jews and Pagans, so, the same feeling was likely afterwards to shew itself, in another form, among those who were characterized as *orthodox* and *catholic* Christians, in contradistinction from Heretics, whose tenets had been condemned by the general voice of the Christian Churches. How strongly this feeling prevailed, and still prevails, in the members of the Romish Church, every one is well aware: but the circumstance to which I wish to direct attention is, in conformity with the views already taken in the present work, that such a feeling is not peculiar to Romanists as such, but originates in our common nature, and consequently is one from which no one who partakes of that nature can be exempt, without perpetual watchfulness. The Mahometans, as is well known, partake largely of this spirit; and even those of them who are habitual transgressors of their law, still flatter themselves that some superior degree of divine favour is reserved for them as " true believers," beyond what can be expected by the best of those who are strangers to the Koran:

while the Author of *our* faith, on the contrary, teaches us that He will reject as utter strangers to Him those who are ready to make their boast in his *Name*, and to plead that they have even " done many mighty works in that *Name:*" and the knowledge of his Gospel He represents as bringing aggravated condemnation to such as do not live a Christian life; since " the servant who knew his Lord's will, and did it not, shall be beaten with many stripes."

§. 3. In order to profit as we may do by the example of the Romanists, and even of the Mahometans, we must waive, for the time, all questions concerning the unsoundness of their tenets, and confine our view to the danger which is common to men of all persuasions, whether essentially correct, or contaminated with more or less of error. If Mahomet had been a true Prophet, as Moses was, this would not have secured his followers from the fault into which the disciples of Moses did in fact fall; viz. that of expecting to be saved by their privileges, rather than by the use made of them. And if the Romanists were following in their system of doctrine and discipline, not the dictates of weak or wicked men, but those of a truly infallible Apostle, this would not alone secure them from the very error which the Apostles themselves found perpetually springing up among their converts, even in their own lifetime; the tendency to substitute the *means* of grace for the *fruits* of grace;—the proud confidence of belonging to a certain holy Community, Church, Sect, or party, which must secure an especial share of divine favour to every member of it.

If, on the contrary, we dwell on the *groundlessness* of the claim of the Romish Church to be the only true and Catholic Church, and on the doctrinal errors into which that Church has fallen, we shall of course be likely to flatter ourselves, as Protestants are apt to do, that our abhorrence of that Church exempts us from all danger of vainly trusting in a Name, and in our connection with a highly-endowed Society.

It is true that the Romish Church has erred in many essential points; but nothing probably has more contributed to lead her into those errors than reliance on Names and Privileges. Spiritual advantages which are *real*, and titles which are *not* misapplied, may be made subjects of presumptuous boast, and may thus lead to indolent security with respect to personal exertion; this is usually the first error men fall into: the second naturally springs out of this carelessness; the name, that is, survives the thing signified;— the advantages are actually lost, either wholly or in part, through a confident reliance on their intrinsic efficacy, without an endeavour to improve them;—the land which was fertile, becomes a desert, through a confident trust that it will ensure wealth to the possessor, while he neglects to till it.

A familiar illustration of the tendency I have been speaking of, is afforded by the parallel case of Academical institutions. To be a member of a learned Body, is regarded as an honour; it affords to the individual, facilities for the acquirement of learning; and, to others, some degree of presumption that he has used his advantages. How many accordingly pride themselves on being members of such a Society, and on the Title which denotes this, while they think little of acquiring the learning and using the advantages, which alone give to the Name, and to the Society, their value.

All this has been strikingly illustrated in the progressive history of the Church of Rome. She was built by Apostles on Jesus Christ, the only true foundation; she was left by them with sound doctrines and pure Christian worship; her members were cautioned by them not to be "high-minded, but fear;" not to rely on the divine favour as a reason for relaxing personal exertions, but as an encouragement to make them; or to exult in their deliverance from heathen superstition, and their adoption in place of the disobedient, to be the people—the chosen people—of God, but to take warning from the example of his mercy combined with severity.

But they were seduced from humble vigilance into a proud and careless reliance on the greatness of their privileges, till they even lost the talent which they had neglected to employ. What was their condition at the close of the Apostles' ministry? They had renounced idolatry;—they worshipped the true God;—they had the sacred Scriptures, the words of eternal life, in their hands for private study, and in their ears, at their religious meetings;—they had the means of grace among them, the Ordinances appointed by Christ, which are strictly called the Sacraments, and public joint worship, itself of a sacramental character;—they had learned to despise and abhor the superstitious offerings, purifications, and other ceremonies of the heathen, and had been taught to trust in the atonement of Christ alone, and to seek for acceptance before God, by being " led by his Spirit." All these were real and inestimable privileges, and gave them just reason for rejoicing (but for rejoicing in trembling gratitude, and not with careless pride) in the deliverance that had been wrought for them—in their happy condition as contrasted with that of their Pagan neighbours.

But their exultation in these advantages led them first to neglect, and in the end to lose, them; their vain confidence in names, led them first to forget, and afterwards to forfeit, the things which the names denoted. Their minds were fixed on what was past—on what had been done for them, and withdrawn from a vigilant attention to the future—from diligence on their part to " make their calling and election sure." Confident in the titles of Christian—of Orthodox—of Catholic—of the Church of God—and careless of living "as *becometh* saints," they trusted that no deadly error could creep into so holy a Community, and adopted, one by one, the very errors (under new names) of the Paganism which had been renounced; thanking God, like the Pharisee, that they were "not as other men are," they became gradually like their heathen ancestors, with the aggravation of having sinned against light, and abused their peculiar advantages; and their confidence all the while increasing along with their carelessness and corruption, when their "gold was become dross," they boasted more than ever of their wealth, and in the midst of their grossest errors insisted on complete infallibility. And to what did all this at length bring them? How far did they ultimately depart from their primitive purity? "How did the faithful city become an harlot?" They ended in overlaying Christianity, one by one, with the very errors and superstitions (in substance) from which the first Christians exulted in being delivered.

Idolatry of the grossest kind was gradually restored: the worshippers of the one true God manifested in Christ Jesus, paid, practically, their chief adoration to deified mortals: the Scriptures were secluded from the people under the veil of an unknown tongue[a], and their interpretation fettered and their authority superseded, even with the learned, by a mass of traditions which made the word of God of none effect; their sacraments became superstitious charms; their public worship a kind of magic incantation muttered in a dead language; and Christian holiness of life was commuted for holy water—for fantastic penances, pilgrimages, amulets, pecuniary donations, and a whole train of superstitious observances, worthy of Paganism in its worst forms. "How is the faithful city become an harlot!" They trusted in Privileges and Names, till the privileges were lost, and the names became an empty sound. But still they are as proud of them as ever. They distinguish themselves by the title of Catholics[b], members of the True Church—adherents to the ancient faith: nay, even *Christians* is a title by which on the Con-

---

[a] A language, be it remembered, which *gradually became* obsolete: for no Church ever *introduced* the use of an unknown tongue, in its prayers, or recital of Scripture.

[b] See note [A] in the Appendix.

tinent they distinguish themselves from those heretics[c], as they term them, who chiefly differ from themselves in trusting in Christ as the One Mediator, instead of a host of pretended saints. Such monstrous corruptions could never have been introduced into any Church by the arts of a worldly and ambitious hierarchy, had not the individual members of it been lulled into a false security, by boastfully contemplating their Christian privileges, instead of dwelling on the additional responsibility these privileges create; by priding themselves on names, without bestowing a watchful attention on the things those names denote.

§. 4. The warning of the Apostle, in his Epistle to this very Church, they neglected, and imitated the very example by which he warned them—that of the presumptuous and disobedient Jews of old. The admonitions, I say, of Paul to the

---

[c] Those in the neighbourhood of the Vandois, in particular, distinguish themselves from the members of that pure and ancient Church, by the distinguishing appellation of Christians.

Church of Rome were lost on the succeeding generations of that Church: shall they be also lost on us? Or shall we say that *Protestants* have no need of them, because we do not trust in the title of Catholic, or in being members of an infallible Church;—because we have protested against the usurpations of that Church, and have renounced her corruptions? The Apostle might reply to us, if he lived in these days, " Be not high-minded, but fear: those whom I then addressed were in the very same situation as you: they were the *reformed*—the Protestants of their day; they had been delivered from Jewish and Pagan infidelity, as you have been from Romish corruptions of Christianity; they prided themselves on that deliverance, as you are liable to do, on yours: they felt confident that they were in no danger of *precisely* the same errors as those of the infidel-Jews and heathen idolaters, and they incorporated into Christianity substantially the same errors, under different names; they have fallen from their first faith; and are left with the candle of God's word darkened, and their minds bewildered by the false light of a delusive superstition: if God spared not this branch, take heed lest He also spare not thee: behold, therefore, the goodness and the severity of God; on them which fell, severity; but toward thee, goodness, if thou continue in his goodness; otherwise thou also shalt be cut off."

The examples which are adduced from the cases of those in different ages and countries from our own, are apt to lose their instructive force, from the very circumstance which ought to make them the more instructive; viz. that there will always be some, if not essential, yet circumstantial, difference between the temptations which arise, and the errors which prevail, among different sets of men. Hence, we are apt to lose sight of the substantial agreement between two cases, and to derive no profit from the recorded faults of others, because those to which we are liable are not the same in name, and in all the accompanying circumstances. Yet this very difference proves that they were not *copied*, the one from the other, but originate in a common and deep-seated source; it would enable us to draw the more instruction from such examples, if we would but remember that man's nature is always, and every where, substantially the same; because we view with a more impartial eye such errors as do not precisely resemble what prevail among ourselves. For these reasons, the backslidings of the Israelites in the wilderness, for instance, are so earnestly set forth by the Apostle, for the instruction of the Corinthians, as being an example likely to be overlooked by them, and especially profitable to be contemplated by them; disposed, as they probably were, to rest in their high privileges as God's people, even as the Israelites did of old, and to think, like them, their deliverance complete, and their attainment of the promised inheritance secure, without watchfulness against the trials that awaited them.

It is with this view, accordingly, that I have attempted, in the present work, to point out what instructive lessons may be drawn from the errors of our brethren of the Romish Church. For when once it is clearly perceived, that her corruptions are such as human nature is prone to—that they are rather the cause, than the effect, of the system of that Church—and that consequently, those out of her pale are not therefore safe from similar corruptions—we are then the more likely to guard watchfully against those faults, whose deformity we have seen fully displayed in another.

§. 5. In pursuing this view, I took occasion to illustrate the general principle, by touching briefly on some of the particular points in which faults, essentially the same with those of the Romanists, have beset, and will ever beset, the rest of mankind also, in proportion as their vigilance against them is remitted: but to enumerate and dwell on all these points, would not only have led to too long a discussion, but would hardly have been needful. For when once the general principle is embraced, it is easy, and it is also best, for every one to follow up for himself the several applications of it, and to pursue the train of thought thus suggested. Nor should this be done once for all, in a single discussion, but, practically, throughout the whole of his Christian life: since if it be fully understood that the system of Romanism, so far as it disagrees with true Christianity, is in fact a transcript of man's frail nature, every one must perceive the necessity of contemplating, as in a mirror, this portraiture of his own infirmities, and of not merely abjuring, once for all, the errors he censures in another, but guarding against them with incessant vigilance. The more secure any one feels against his liability to errors, to which in fact he *is* liable, the greater must be his real danger of falling into them.

In pointing out, accordingly, several particular classes of faults to which Protestants are liable, and which are substantially the same as they condemn in the Romanists, I have repeatedly dwelt on that aggravation of the danger, the false security we are likely to feel, in our renunciation of the Papal dominion, against the errors of Romanism. I cannot therefore more properly conclude this treatise, than by observing, that this very *false security* is itself one of the most fatal of those errors;—that we are in fact imitating the Romanists, if we securely exult in our separation from them:—if we trust in the name of Protestant, as they do in that of Catholic; and look back, with proud satisfaction, on our emancipation from their corrupt system, without also looking forward, to guard vigilantly against the like corruptions; even as *they* triumphed in their abandonment of Pagan superstitions, while they forgot that Paganism itself was the offspring of the self-deceiving heart of man, in which the same corruptions, if not watchfully repressed, will be continually springing up afresh.

A more acceptable subject, perhaps, I might easily have found, in exposing the enormities of the Church of Rome, and panegyrizing the comparative purity of our own; inasmuch as self-congratulation is more agreeable than self-examination. But with a view to our own practical improvement, there can be no doubt which is the more profitable. The Apostle's warning, "be not high-minded, but fear," was not likely to be so gratifying to the Church of Rome, to which it was addressed, as unmixed praise and congratulation; but it would have saved them, had they continued duly to attend to it, from the evils which it denounced.

Let the Protestant then consider their fall as recorded " for his admonition:" and let him profit by the example before him.

The errors which, with these views, I selected for consideration, as being among the most prominent, and usually regarded as most characteristic, of the Romish Church[d], but which I have endeavoured to trace to our common Nature, are, 1. Superstition; considered as consisting, not in this or that particular mode of worship, but in *misdirected* religious veneration, generally: 2. the tendency towards what may be called a vicarious service of God; a proneness to convert the Christian Minister into a Priest in the other sense of the word, and to substitute his sanctity of life and devotion, for those of the people: 3. the toleration of what are called " pious frauds;" either in the sacrifice of truth to supposed expediency, or in the propagation of what is believed to be the truth, by dishonest artifice: 4. an undue deference to Human Authority; as, in other points, so especially in forgetting the legitimate use of creeds, catechisms, liturgies, and other such compositions set forth by any Church, and intruding them gradually into the place of Scripture, by habitually appealing to them (where the appeal ought always to be made to the records of inspiration) in *proof* of any doctrine that is in question: which practice I pointed out as not originally the

[d] See Appendix [B.]

consequence, but the cause, of the claim to inspiration and infallibility set up by the Church: 5. Lastly, I remarked, that Intolerance, or the spirit of Persecution, i. e. the disposition to enforce by secular coercion, not, this or that system of religion, but, one's *own*, whatever it may be, is a fault inherent in human nature, and to which consequently all mankind are liable, however strongly they may reprobate (as, e. g. the Romish Church has always done) persecution, or any form of compulsion, exercised on themselves[e].

From these then, and all other Romish errors, Protestants cannot, as such, be exempt; and they are in the greater danger of them in proportion to their abhorrence of them as existing in that Church, if they regard them as properly the offspring of Romanism, and not of human nature;—if they build their security on their being out of the pale of that corrupt Church, and neglect to guard against the spirit of those corruptions, while they exult in the Name of Protestants. This careless reliance on Titles and Privileges, is, as I have in this chapter been endeavouring to shew, itself one of the most mischievous of the

[e] See Appendix [B.]

Romish errors, and which has mainly contributed to favour the introduction of the rest.

§. 6. In what way then, it may be asked, are we to apply practically what has been said, in guarding against this particular error? Let any one (I would reply) but look around him, and look within his own heart. Are there not multitudes who exult in the title of Christian— of Protestant—of Churchman—and in their belonging to a Society endowed with such high privileges? There are: and would God the description, thus far, were even more universally applicable than it is; for in these things we *ought* to rejoice, even much more than we do. But do all who congratulate themselves on these advantages, and on these names, and who regard it, if not as some sort of merit, at least, as a sure pledge of some divine favour, to possess them—do all of these reflect on the superior responsibility which is thus imposed on them? Do none of them (in feelings and in conduct at least, though not in express avowal) cherish a hope of being saved by their privileges, rather than by the use made of them? Do they reflect on those privileges as aggravating their condemnation if they do not rightly use them; or do they exult in their admittance to the wedding-feast, forgetful that the guest who " had not put on the wedding-garment," was cast " into outer darkness?" Do they regard the names of Christian and of Protestant as a *reproach* to those who bear them, if they are not " led by the Spirit of Christ"—if they do not in their heart and life, as well as with their lips, *protest* against the faults which they condemn in the Romanists?

Nor is it to the names of *Christian* and of *Protestant* alone, that these cautions will apply: every title which we claim that implies any peculiar advantage, involves a corresponding responsibility; and a corresponding danger, if we forget that responsibility. Does any one consider himself entitled to the name of Churchman—of Orthodox—of Evangelical?—let him remember, that there is a perpetual danger of his relying, in proud security on these titles—of trusting, not so much to his endeavours after personal holiness, as to the sanctity of the society, sect, or party, with which he is thus connected.

Some members of the Romish Church, not satisfied with merely belonging to that Church, and with the title of Catholics, have enrolled themselves in certain subordinate Societies, (or Religious Orders as they are called,) enlisting themselves under the banner of some founder, of supposed superior sanctity. I am not now enquiring into the peculiar errors and superstitions actually connected with these institutions: had they been exempt from every thing of this kind, there would still have been a danger (which, in fact, must exist, more or less, in all religious Communities whatever) of that evil which has so notoriously attended the Religious Societies of the Romish Church:—the evil, I mean, of considering the mutual connection of the members of such Societies as a kind of *partnership;* in which each member may hope to derive *some* benefit at least, from the piety and purity of the whole Body. This absurdity—the supposed transfer of the merits of one sinful mortal to the account of another—has indeed never been distinctly avowed except in the Church of Rome: but the tendency towards such a feeling must have been inherent in the Human Heart, or men never could have been brought to acknowledge it. The danger of it, is, as I have said, inherent in the very nature of a religious *Community*. As, in a Partnership, the neglect of one man may often be in some degree remedied by the diligence of others; and as, in an Army, the soldier who does not himself fight bravely, may sometimes, through the valour of his comrades and the skill of his general, be made partaker of the benefits, and sometimes even of the glory, of a victory; so, men are apt to transfer views thus familiar to them, to the case of Members of a *Religious* Society. And this danger, being, as I have said, one which necessarily besets *every* religious Society, can never be escaped except by incessant vigilance. For Christianity is essentially a social Religion. We are " every one members one of another;" and the Author of our Faith has decreed, that Christians are to further their own salvation, by labouring jointly to forward the salvation of each other. But it is by the personal faith and holiness of *each* individual Christian, that each individual Christian, after all, is to be made, through the intercession of the *one* Mediator and Redeemer, whose Spirit sanctifies his heart, acceptable before God. The pious labours of others can do nothing for any man, unless they lead him to labour in like manner for himself.

Richly endowed indeed is the Church of Christ with the *means* of Grace—with *privileges* and advantages of inestimable value; but if we fail to *use* these means, and to *avail* ourselves of these privileges, they will but increase our condemnation. The name of Christian—of Reformed, of Protestant Christian—instead of saving, will condemn, as doubly inexcusable, on the great day, when the secrets of men's hearts shall be disclosed, him, who, " naming the name of Christ," has not " departed from iniquity;"—who " heareth his words, and doeth them not;"—whose life and heart are not " reformed"—and who exults over the errors of the Romish Church, while he supinely overlooks those evil propensities of our common nature, from which they took their rise. " For he is not a Jew," (nor, by parity of reasoning, a Christian—an Orthodox, or an Evangelical Christian—a Reformed, or a Protestant Christian,) " who is one outwardly, neither is that circumcision which is outward in the flesh; but he is a Jew, who is one inwardly; and circumcision is that of the heart, in the spirit, and not in the letter; whose praise is not of men, but of God."

APPENDIX.

[A.]

THE title of *Catholics*, the Romanists claim, and apply to themselves, not merely as *belonging* to them, (and it is not denied that they are a branch, though a corrupt one, of the Universal or Catholic Church,) but as *distinctive*, and peculiar to the members of the Church of Rome. And Protestants have usually, in language, conceded this claim. But, I think, that in so doing, they manifest too exclusively the harmlessness of the dove, and leave the wisdom of the serpent entirely with their opponents. It is urged, that these are offended at being called Pápists; considering that as a term of reproach, from its being used only by their adversaries. That I may not seem to seek a quarrel, I have generally avoided that name: but let us not be so weak as to imagine, that " Romanist," or any other title by which they can be, *properly*, designated, will ever fail, *when it shall have become common*, to be complained of as reproachful; or that they will ever acquiesce in any appellation which does not *imply a reproach to ourselves*. Even the apparently neutral designation of "Members of the Church of Rome," is one which we must not too confidently expect them to adopt or acquiesce in; nor is it unlikely that they may complain of it as reproachful, should it ever become their customary appellation among Protestants. For it implies, that there are *other* Churches, properly called Churches, besides the Church of Rome. *We* indeed are content to be designated as Members of the Church of England; and we regard them as belonging to a distinct Church, over which, though we censure it as corrupt, we claim no supremacy; but they do not take a corresponding view of us: they do not regard us as constituting *any* distinct Church, but as actually members, though schismatical and revolted members—subjects, de jure, though rebellious subjects—of *their Church*. A name therefore which implies, that there *are* other Churches distinct from theirs, contradicts one of their fundamental tenets; viz. that they, and they only, are faithful members of the one true Church. And this tenet they have embodied in the appellation they have chosen for themselves; which consequently implies, as I have said, a reproach to all other Christians. The title of Catholic, when used as distinctive, implies the exclusion of all others from the character of loyal members of the Society which Christ founded—of " the holy Catholic Church, the Communion of Saints," as it is expressed and explained in the Apostles' Creed: it implies, in short, that all others are heretics or schismatics.

This is no uncommon device. There is a sect who call themselves "Baptists," i. e. persons who *baptize*; thus implying that no others are *really* baptized, and that infant-baptism is null and void. This is their distinctive tenet; which they are perfectly right in professing, if convinced of its truth: but it is an absurdity for any one who differs from them to give them this title, which palpably begs the question at issue, and condemns himself. The title of Antipædobaptist is to be sure somewhat cumbrous; but awkwardness of expression, or even circumlocution, is preferable to error and absurdity. " The same caution might well be extended to the use of the word *Unitarian*, as the title of a sect; for the term properly expresses a fundamental doctrine which the Church holds. *Socinian* appears to me a better appellation. But this too I would avoid, if it gave serious offence; at the same time, being careful to make it known that the word *Unitarian* is employed in compliance with a custom, which however general, and perhaps harmless, I cannot but regard as objectionable [a]."

That the term Papist is a term of reproach, (though I do not insist on its being employed,) I can never admit. A " term of reproach" is *one which implies*

[a] Note to Bishop Copleston's Sermon at the re-opening of Abergavenny Church.

something disgraceful in the opinion of the party to whom it is applied. Thus, Heretic (in its ordinary, not perhaps in its etymological, sense) implies the holding of some *erroneous* tenet; it is, consequently, a reproachful term. But Papist implies simply one who *acknowledges the authority of the Pope:* and those to whom it is applied, do, openly, acknowledge his authority.

" Considering the tendency of *words*" (says a writer whom I am proud to appeal to) " to influence *opinions*, I hold the right use of this word CATHOLIC to be of essential importance. The controversial writers of the Church of Rome never fail to take advantage of the want of caution in this respect observable among Protestants. Of this a strong example is given in a recent publication, which affords a gratifying proof of the strength of our cause, and of the weakness of the Romanists, whenever they are respectively brought to the test of Scripture and of reason. I allude to the correspondence between the Clergy of Blackburn and the Principal and other members of the Roman Catholic establishment at Stonyhurst. From this interesting publication I cannot do better than extract the following passage in one of Mr. Whittaker's letters to the Principal of that institution.

' It was not from a love of contending about words, still less from any reluctance to give every possible satisfaction to the Romish priesthood, that I persisted in refusing the unqualified term " Catholic" to them and their Church. The use which they make of it, when it is conceded to them, cannot be unknown to you. Dr. Milner, in his End of Religious Controversy, (Letter XXV.) says of our Church, " Every time they address the God of truth, either in solemn worship or in private devotion, they are forced each of them to repeat, *I believe in* THE CATHOLIC CHURCH, and yet, if I ask any of them the question, *are you a* CATHOLIC? he is sure to answer me, *No! I am a* PROTESTANT!!—Was there ever a more glaring instance of inconsistency and self-condemnation among rational beings?"—" But," says one of the Blackburn Secular Priests to me, " where is the man that can or will accuse you of acting inconsistently with your religious principles," supposing me to concede this appellation to their Church and its members exclusively? I refer him for his answer to Dr. Milner, with whom I entirely agree, that a more glaring instance of inconsistency and self-condemnation " cannot well exist among rational beings," than that exhibited by Protestants, who confess before God that they believe in His Holy Catholic Church, and allow themselves to limit the practical use of the term to the Church of Rome.'—*Correspondence, &c. published at Blackburn,* 1829, p. 14.

" There is nothing I abhor more than religious persecution—nothing I would censure more strongly than a wanton offence given to the feelings of others, on account of a sincere difference in religious opinion.

Yet I cannot carry this principle so far as to abstain from calling the members of that Church who refuse to join in our reformation of its errors, by some appellation which marks their adherence to its communion, and their submission to its authority. *Papist* appears to me the most correct designation, because the differences in doctrine are often ingeniously softened down and even explained away by the more enlightened Roman Catholics, but I never met with one who did not hold that spiritual submission to the bishop of Rome in some sense or other was indispensable. The word Papist, however, is understood by them as a reproach. Let us then, in Christian charity, forbear to use it. But some phrase indicative of their connexion with Rome, and of their dependence upon the authority of that see, whether Romish, or Romanist, or Roman Catholic, I hold to be not only allowable, but highly expedient, and even necessary: and heartily do I wish that all Protestants would form themselves to a habit of thus speaking, both in public and private: for it then would never be understood as a personal affront, but as a serious and firm resolution not to compliment away an important point, in which *our* feelings and *our* honour are at least as much concerned as *theirs*[b]."

" Yes but" (I have heard it answered) " the term Papist implies more than mere submission to Papal supremacy; it implies the adoption of an *erroneous*

[b] Bp. Copleston's Sermon at Abergavenny, p. 23, 24.

system and submission to an *usurped* authority." It implies no such thing. That indeed is *my opinion* respecting the Romish system; but the *word* does not denote that. The difference is practically very great and important, between a word which itself *expresses error or wrong*, and a word which denotes some *thing* which the speaker *believes* to be erroneous or wrong. One person, for instance, may think a democracy the best form of government, and another may think it the worst; the one will consequently have the most pleasing, the other the most odious, associations with the term Democrat; but the word itself is not used by them in two different senses; it expresses simply, an " advocate for democracy;" and it is not, in itself, either a term of honour or of reproach. On the other hand, " patriot" and " traitor" imply, respectively, honour and dishonour, in their very signification.

Inattention to this obvious distinction leads to endless confusion of thought and practical perplexity. If every term is to be reckoned reproachful, which is associated in the mind of him who uses it with some odious or contemptible idea, then, the title of *Catholic* will itself be such, when applied by Protestants to designate the Church of Rome. *Every* term, in short, will be a term of reproach when used by one who disapproves the opinion, system, or party, implied by it. The Mahometans associate with the title of *Christian* every thing that is hateful or despicable; shall we then complain or be ashamed of being called Christians? " God forbid that we should glory, save in the cross of our Lord Jesus Christ." Mahometan, again, is a title which recalls to the Christian the idea of " disciple of an impostor;" but the title itself does not imply Mahomet's being either a false or a true prophet; and *they* accordingly do not regard it as a reproachful title.

But the term Christian *would* be reproachful if applied *by one Mahometan to another*; because it expresses something which that other holds in abhorrence. So also the title of Mahometan would be a reproach if applied to a Christian; and Papist, again, for the same reason, is a term of reproach, if applied to one who professes himself a Protestant. An appellation, in short, is or is not reproachful, according to the professed tenets, *not of him who applies it*, but of him *to whom it is applied*. To be called a Papist, (i. e. " one who admits the Pope's authority,") is a reproach to him who does not, and none to him who does, profess that principle.

But we are told, that the term is used by none but the adversaries of the Romanists, and therefore they have a right to complain of it. At this rate they may *make* any title they will, a term of reproach, by simply refusing to apply it to themselves. And we may be assured they *will* do so with *every* title which *does not imply a reproach to us*. To call themselves, distinctively Catholics, is (as *they* at least are well aware, whatever we may be) to call *us* heretics. Let them be admonished, that when they except against the name of Papists, and assume that of Catholics, declaiming at the same time against the cruelty of using reproachful language—let them be admonished, that the censure applies, not to us, but to themselves.

And let it not be thought that this is a trifling " question of words and names :" it was a wise maxim, laid down and skilfully acted on by some of the leaders of the French Revolution, that " names are things." Great is the practical effect in all debate and controversy, of suffering to pass unnoticed and to become established, such terms as beg the question, and virtually imply a decision on one side. I remember to have met with a Romanist (by no means bigoted) of the middle class of society, with whom I had a good deal of discussion of the points wherein we differed. What seemed to dwell most on his mind was, the inconsistency, as he deemed it, of our professing belief in " the Holy Catholic Church;" when " yours," he said, " is *not* the Catholic Church."

[B.]

Different persons will, of course, be chiefly struck by different faults, among those charged on the Romanists. Many, for instance, would place foremost one which I have not noticed under a distinct head, and to which they give the title of " self-righteousness." The word does not perhaps savour of the purest English[e]; but what they mean is, a confident trust in the *merit* of our own good-works, as sufficient to *earn* eternal happiness, and as entitling us to that as a just reward.

The Romish Church, however, has not in reality ever set this forth as one of her distinct tenets. If any one will consult, what is of decisive authority in that Church, the decrees of the Council of Trent, he will perceive, that though they may perhaps have made an injudicious use of the word " merit," the abstract question between them and others (not Antinomians) is chiefly verbal. For they admit, and solemnly declare, that nothing we can do can be acceptable before God except for the sake of Jesus Christ; and that we are unable to perform good works except by his Spirit working in us: so that what is called a Christian's righteousness, is, at the same time, the righteousness of Christ, although the Scriptures promise, repeatedly and plainly, that it will, through his goodness, not " lose its reward."

That part of their theory which is the most objectionable on this score, is the doctrine, that from the pains of

---

[e] According to the analogy of the other similar compounds in our language, such as " self-love," " self-condemnation," self-tormentor," &c. " self-righteousness" should signify, upright dealing in respect of one's self.

Purgatory, Christ has not redeemed us, but we are to be rescued either by Penances done in this life, or by Masses offered in our behalf after our death.

But I do think, that, in practice, the Romish system tends to foster the error in question; not so much, however, by the use of the words "merit," and "reward," as by the importance attached to the *actual performance* of a vast multitude of specific works, many of them arbitrarily prescribed, such as abstinence from particular meats on particular days, repetition of "Ave Marys" and "Pater-nosters"—pilgrimages—crossings, &c. which have a manifest tendency to absorb the attention in the *act* itself—to draw off the mind from the endeavour after inward purity—and to create the feeling so congenial to our Nature, that we have been so far advancing in the performance of something *intrinsically* capable of forwarding our salvation.

It is worth remarking, that the great heathen moralist, who understood more of the character of Christian virtue than many Christians do, dwells strongly on the principle, that while, in the Arts, *the thing produced* is what we chiefly look to, in moral action, on the contrary, the frame of mind of the *agent* is the principal point; virtuous *actions* being only the means, though the necessary means, of *making* him, and of *proving* him to be, (what is to be the ultimate object sought after,) an habitually good *man*[d]. But it is an easier task for Man,

[d] See Arist. Eth. b. ii.

such as he is by nature, to conform his outward actions to a certain precisely-fixed *rule*, and to applaud himself for that conformity, than, by incessant vigilance and self-examination, to rectify and regulate the inward character[e].

It is a great mistake, however, to imagine, that Protestants, even those who are the forwardest in condemning this particular kind of Spiritual-Pride, called by them "self-righteousness," are therefore exempt from the danger of Spiritual-Pride altogether. On the contrary, one may find but too plain symptoms of the same disease, even in some who the most abhor and condemn all reliance on the merit of good works. For Pride is too natural an inmate of the human heart to be effectually excluded by being merely "at *one* entrance quite shut out." There are some, as I have above remarked[f], who substitute an unerring Party for an unerring Church, or renounce the shackles of Papal infallibility, as it were in a spirit of rivalry, that they may become, each, a Pope to himself. And these will commonly be found to have merely changed the form, not the substance, of Spiritual-Pride. One may sometimes hear a man professing himself the chief of sinners—proclaiming his own righteousness to be filthy rags—calling himself a brand plucked out of the burning—resting his confidence of salvation wholly on the Atonement of his Redeemer, and on the imputation to himself of the righteous works performed

[e] See Essays V. and VIII. Second Series.   [f] Chap. IV.

by Christ[g]—and acknowledging that he has received every thing from God's free and unmerited bounty; and thence fully trusting that he must have completely attained Christian humility; at least, as far as he does completely adhere to his profession, that whatever he possesses is due to the free grace of God. On this ground we may conceive the Pharisee in the Parable to have congratulated himself on his *humility* as well as his other virtues; since he exclaims, in pious gratitude, " God, *I thank Thee*, that I am not as other men are!" But the Pharisee, it will be answered, rested on his good works—his scrupulous fasting, and paying of tithes. Is there then *no other* conceivable Spiritual-Pride than precisely that of the Pharisees? no other subject of excessive self-confidence and self-congratulation? If there be, it is evident that we cannot, any more than the Pharisee, be exempted from the danger, by merely acknowledging, (as he did) that all we have is the gift of God. And in fact, it may too often be found, that a Christian, who renounces the Romish tenets respecting good works, and who abhors the very name of "merit" as applied to himself or to other men, will have renounced boasting, only in words, and will be full of the most overweening confidence in his own gifts and graces. For there is a striking resemblance between the Romanist and the fanatical Pietist, in their each craving after, (though from different quarters,) and each in

[g] See Essay VI. Second Series.

consequence flattering himself as having attained, some such *definite and certain assurance*, the one from his Church, the other from his feelings, as may finally supersede hesitation and self-distrust—destroy the true nature and value of faith—and deprive the present Life of its character as a state of *discipline*. As the one accordingly relies in proud security on his unerring Church, so the other will proclaim himself enlightened throughout, as to the whole Gospel-scheme, by the divine Spirit; and so far he is right, that the aid of the Holy Spirit *is* promised us to " help our infirmities," and that without this help sought and granted, the clearest intellectual powers will leave a man bewildered, or ill-satisfied. But he who honestly avails himself of this promise, and is truly " led by the Spirit," will be filled, with gratitude indeed for the past, and with cheering hope for the future, but with no arrogant self-confidence, or uncharitable disdain. Without entering into any minute discussion (for which this is not the place[g]) of the different kinds and degrees of spiritual assistance, it is evident that all such enlightening of the mind, either is, or is not, of such a character as to amount to *inspiration*, and imply infallibility. If in any case a man is convinced that he has *not* any claim to this, he ought, in *some* way or other, to manifest that conviction, and to shew that he makes allowance for this difference: if he does reckon himself, properly, inspired,

[g] See Essay IX. Second Series.

he ought at least not to censure the Romish Church for the presumptuous *arrogance* of her claim, but honestly to join issue on the question, whether they or he are *justified* in such a claim: a question which, it appears to me, can only be settled by the performance of sensible miracles.

And I cannot but think the Romanists have the advantage in point of consistency over many modern fanatics, inasmuch as their Church does acknowledge the reasonableness of such an appeal, and claim miraculous powers. But one may find in some Protestants, while they pretend to no such powers, and abjure all arrogant assumption, a decided pretension, if not always expressed in words, at least implied in the whole tenor of their language, to inspiration, properly so called. They state their own views of religion with no less oracular dogmatism than the Romanists;—they bestow no less unhesitating and unsparing censure on all who do not coincide in these views, or who do not, to the minutest tittle, conform to their phraseology in expressing them;—and they look down with the same pharisaical and self-sufficient contempt on every one who does not adopt the notions which they (as they often express themselves) have been taught by the Spirit of God. And if any one remains unconvinced by their arguments, or by their assertions instead of argument, or if he meet these with such objections as they are at a loss to answer, they will in general boldly and promptly resort to the cheap expedient of pronouncing him incapable of comprehending the subject, from being in an unregenerate state: for " the natural man receiveth not the things that are of God;" and such, they conclude at once, must be the condition of any one who disallows, or, still more, who refutes, their opinions, which they are sure are the " things of God." Any, the slightest, departure from the standard of their (as it might be called, in analogy to their own phraseology) " Self-Infallibility," is regarded by them as a decisive proof of entire spiritual blindness.

But still, inasmuch as they abhor " self-righteousness," claiming no merit whatsoever for their own good works, and pretending *only* to the character of the peculiarly-favoured and inspired people of God, they flatter themselves that they are quite safe from spiritual-pride; and thus they complete their presumptuous confidence, by adding to the list of their other perfections, the perfect attainment of genuine Christian Humility. Being utter strangers to self-distrust and humble vigilance, they feel, for this very reason, the more secure against any deficiency of these; and the very completeness of their spiritual-pride, makes them the more completely confident of being wholly free from it.

If such be, as I fear it is, but too true a picture of the language and tone of feeling which may not unfrequently be met with, even among those who not only condemn the arrogance of the Romish plea of merit, but are sedulous in warning Protestants against the like sin, this furnishes a strong, and afflicting, and awful instance of a delusion by which our spiritual enemy can obtrude upon us some vice, dressed up in the very garb of the opposite virtue, even at the very time when we are occupied in the most vehement reprobation of it: while we are, in one point, scrupulous to " strain off the gnat," and in another, ready to " swallow the camel."

Never will the sin of spiritual-pride more easily beset us, than under the guise of a self-abhorring humility. And never will the preacher be more successful in making (apparent) converts, than when he is unconsciously flattering the evil propensities of man's corrupt nature, while he appears to repress them. " It is sometimes considered as a proof of the advantage to be obtained from the habit which I am here presuming to discourage, that such preaching generally proves attractive to the lower classes. This, however, may be accounted for, without furnishing any justification of the practice. For, first, the lower classes, unless they are truly religious, usually *are* gross sinners, and, therefore, are neither surprised nor shocked at being supposed so themselves, and at the same time feel a sort of pleasure which need not be encouraged, when they hear their superiors brought down to the same level: and, secondly, it seems to furnish them with a sort of excuse for their sins, to find that they are so universal, and so much to be expected of human nature[h]." Nothing indeed is more

[h] Sumner, Apostolical Preaching, p. 133.

likely to be popular, and less likely to be profitable, than to act the part of the Stoic philosopher to Damasippus; (Hor. Sat. iii. b. 2.) who assured him that he need not feel any shame at his own follies, at least as compared with those of other men [i], since all except the true wise-men [k] were equally foolish and insane [l], though in various ways; and that he had only to enroll himself in this privileged and enlightened philosophical Sect, adopt the maxims of his new school [m], and immediately look down with disdain on those he had been accustomed to look up to with a mixture of reverence, envy, despair, and dislike [n].

The whole of this admirable Satire is well worth a re-perusal, with a view to the present subject, for the sake of the light it throws on the substantial identity, under the most different forms and names, of human nature in all ages and countries.

[i] . . . . . . hoc te
Credo modo insanum; nihilo ut sapientior ille
Qui te deridet. Sat. iii. b. ii. l. 51.

[k] . . Hæc populos, hæc magnos formula reges,
Excepto sapiente, tenet. l. 45.

[l] It should be remembered, that the *equality of all faults* was a favourite doctrine of the Stoics.

[m] . . . . . . unde ego mira
Descripsi docilis præcepta hæc, tempore quo me
Solatus jussit sapientem pascere barbam,
Atque a Fabricio non tristem ponte reverti. l. 34.

[n] . . . . . . amico
Arma dedit, posthac ne compellarer inultus. l. 297.

It ever must have been, and ever will be, a far more irksome task to Human Nature, to drink, drop by drop, the medicine, so bitter to the " Natural Man," of self-abasement, than to get rid of the potion in a single draught;—to weed out, one by one, deep-rooted habits, and gradually to retrace his steps by daily perseverance, than to leap at once to a secure eminence, from which he may look back, in the exultation of superiority, on those whose greater forwardness in the Christian course he had been used to regard with almost hopeless mortification.

Well therefore may we expect, that those who are not sedulously on their guard, will be often seduced by a temptation which addresses itself at once to the impatient indolence, to the jealousy, and to the pride, of the human heart.

To the topics I have touched on in the course of this Work, I might have added, besides many others, some allusion to the re-introduction among some Protestants of *Auricular Confession*, though so far modified as not to be made to a *priest*; by which alteration, I conceive, both the *good*, in some instances, and the *evil*, in many more, of the Romish practice, is diminished. That good as well as evil—beneficial as well as pernicious effects—have been produced by auricular Confession, I have not a doubt. And this perhaps has had its share in the wide diffusion, long continuance, and partial restoration of the practice. But the chief cause is, I am convinced, (as in the case of the other Romish practices,) that there is a natural craving in mankind for this unburdening of the conscience, by confession to a fellow-creature. The Romish system has taken advantage of this, by misinterpreting the scriptural recommendation, to "confess our sins one to another," as a *requisition* of a *regular* and *complete* periodical Confession, making a portion of Christian discipline. And the practice so established, whether with Romanists or Protestants, I am convinced does evil ten times oftener, and of ten thousand times greater magnitude, than good: nor can I but regard it as, practically, one of the very worst parts of Romanism. Indeed, my chief reason for not dwelling on it further is, that I *could not*, with propriety, exhibit it in its true colours, or describe what I not only believe, but, I may say, know*, respecting its effects.

Enough however has been said on several points, and perhaps more than enough for minds disposed to follow up a principle in its several applications, to shew the necessity of unceasing vigilance, and, not indeed of often-repeated thorough *reformations*, (which are always

---

* See Dedication.

attended with more or less evil,) but, of such perpetual revision, renovation, purification, and progressive *improvement*, in every system, as shall supersede the necessity of great changes; such constant attention to keep every thing, as it were, in good *repair*, that there shall be no need of totally pulling down and rebuilding.

But there is an error common to many of those who in other respects vary infinitely in their views; to many, both of the adherents of the unreformed Romish Church, with its long-accumulated load of abuses; and of those who are fully satisfied with the system of some reformed Church; and again of those who advocate further reform, from the most extravagant, to the most moderate. The error, I mean, of conceiving a system, whether actually existing, or ideal, so framed, as to *keep itself in good order*;—one that either is, or may be, so wisely constituted as to remain perfect, or as near as is possible to perfection, without any call for incessantly-watchful care on our part. This error, I say, is common to men of the most opposite views. Some attribute this character to the Church of Rome, as founded by the Apostles; or to some Protestant Church, as reformed by Luther or Calvin; resigning themselves to tranquil security against all but external dangers, and apprehending none but sudden and violent innovations; forgetful of the wise remark of Bacon, that "Time is the greatest innovator; though his changes creep in so quietly as to escape notice [p]." Others, on the contrary, see numberless defects, real or imaginary, in these Churches, and wish for a total, or for a partial, change: still flattering themselves, like their opponents, that a system once established on their principles, will continue, without further care or vigilance, to answer all its purposes for ever;—in short, that the machine will go right, if undisturbed, without ever needing to be regulated, or to be wound up. Never let it be forgotten then, that we are beset by the same truly chimerical hope, in human affairs, which has misled so many speculators in Mechanics; the vain expectation of attaining the PERPETUAL MOTION.

[p] " Novator maximus, Tempus . . . . quod novationes ita insinuat ut sensus fallant."

THE END.

BAXTER, PRINTER, OXFORD.

BOOKS PRINTED FOR
B. FELLOWES, LUDGATE STREET.

SERMONS, preached in the Parish Church of St. Botolph, Bishopsgate. By C. J. BLOMFIELD, D.D. Rector, now Bishop of London. Second Edition. 8vo. 12s.

TWELVE LECTURES on the ACTS of the APOSTLES; to which is added, a new Edition of FIVE LECTURES on the GOSPEL of St. JOHN. By C. J. BLOMFIELD, D.D. Bishop of London. Second Edition. 8vo. 10s. 6d.

A SERMON, preached before the King's Most Excellent Majesty, in the Chapel Royal at St. James's, on Sunday, July 4, 1830. By CHARLES JAMES, Lord Bishop of London, Dean of His Majesty's Chapels Royal. Published by His Majesty's Command. 4to. 2s.

A CHARGE, delivered to the CLERGY of his Diocese, by CHARLES JAMES, Lord Bishop of London, at his Primary Visitation in July, 1830. 4to. 2s. 6d.

A LETTER on the PRESENT NEGLECT of the LORD'S DAY, addressed to the Inhabitants of London and Westminster. By C. J. BLOMFIELD, D.D. Bishop of London. Seventh Edition. 8vo. 1s.

ESSAYS on SOME of the DIFFICULTIES in the WRITINGS of St. PAUL, and in other parts of the New Testament. By RICHARD WHATELY, D.D. Principal of St. Alban's Hall, Oxford. Second Edition, with Additions. 8vo. 10s.

A VIEW of the SCRIPTURE REVELATIONS concerning A FUTURE STATE, laid before his Parishioners. By A COUNTRY PASTOR. Second Edition. 12mo. 5s. 6d.

HISTORIC DOUBTS relative to NAPOLEON BUONAPARTE. Third Edition. 8vo. 2s.

Books printed for B. Fellowes.

A SHORT ACCOUNT of the FIRST PREACHING of THE GOSPEL by the APOSTLES, being a continuation of "Conversations on the Life of Jesus Christ." By a Mother. 18mo. nearly ready.

REMARKS on some of the CHARACTERS of SHAKSPEARE. By T. WHATELY, Esq. Second Edition, edited by REV. RICHARD WHATELY, D.D. 12mo. 4s.

ESSAYS on the LIVES of COWPER, NEWTON, and HEBER; or an Examination of the Evidence of the Course of Nature being interrupted by the Divine Government. 8vo. 10s.

THE CATECHIST'S MANUAL and FAMILY LECTURER; being an Arrangement and Explanation of St. Mark's Gospel, for purposes of Missionary and Domestic Instruction. By the REV. SAMUEL HINDS, M.A. of Queen's College, and Vice-Principal of St. Alban's Hall, Oxford. 8vo. 10s. 6d.

THE THREE TEMPLES of the ONE TRUE GOD contrasted. By the REV. SAMUEL HINDS, M.A. &c. &c. 8vo. 5s. 6d.

The HISTORY of the RISE and EARLY PROGRESS of CHRISTIANITY. By the Rev. SAMUEL HINDS, M.A. &c. &c. 2 vols. 8vo. 1l. 1s.

ELEMENTS of LOGIC. By R. WHATELY, D.D. Principal of St. Alban's Hall, Oxford. Third Edition. 8vo. 12s.

REFLECTIONS on the DECLINE of SCIENCE in ENGLAND, and on some of its Causes. By CHARLES BABBAGE, Esq. Lucasian Professor of Mathematics in the University of Cambridge, &c. 8vo. 7s. 6d.

A COMPARATIVE VIEW of the DIFFERENT INSTITUTIONS for the ASSURANCE of LIVES. By CHARLES BABBAGE, Esq. 8vo. 10s. 6d.

TABLE of LOGARITHMS of the NATURAL NUMBERS, from 1 to 108,000. By CHARLES BABBAGE, Esq. Royal 8vo. 12s.

TABLES of LOGARITHMIC SINES, COSINES, TANGENTS, and COTANGENTS, to accompany Mr. Babbage's Table of Logarithms. Royal 8vo. 12s.

Books printed for B. Fellowes.

The ELEMENTS of ALGEBRA; designed for the Use of Students in the University. By JAMES WOOD, D.D. Dean of Ely, and Master of St. John's College, Cambridge. 8vo. 7s.

The PRINCIPLES of MECHANICS. By JAMES WOOD, D.D. &c. 8vo. 5s.

The ELEMENTS of OPTICS. By JAMES WOOD, D.D. &c. 8vo. 6s.

ÆSCHYLI AGAMEMNON, a BLOMFIELD. Editio Tertia. 8vo. 12s.

ÆSCHYLI CHOEPHORŒ, a BLOMFIELD. Editio Secunda. 8vo. 8s.

ÆSCHYLI PERSÆ, a BLOMFIELD. Editio Quarta. 8vo. 8s.

ÆSCHYLI PROMETHEUS, a BLOMFIELD. Editio Quinta. 8vo. 8s.

ÆSCHYLI SEPTEM CONTRA THEBAS, a BLOMFIELD. Editio Quarta. 8vo. 8s.

An INDEX to the GLOSSARIES contained in BISHOP BLOMFIELD'S Edition of ÆSCHYLUS. By a Graduate of the University of Oxford. 8vo. 3s.

EURIPIDIS HIPPOLYTUS CORONIFER, a MONK. Editio Quarta. 8vo. 7s.

EURIPIDIS ALCESTIS, a MONK. Editio Quarta. 8vo. 6s.

EURIPIDIS TROADES, accedit SEIDLERI, MATTHIÆ, et Aliorum Annotatio Selecta, cui et pauca quædam sua subjecit Editor. 8vo. 7s. 6d.

A GRAMMAR of the LATIN LANGUAGE. By C. G. ZUMPT, Professor in the University of Berlin. Translated from the German, with Additions, by the Rev. JOHN KENRICK, M.A. Second Edition, corrected and enlarged. 8vo. 10s. 6d.

.... " Far superior to any existing Grammar that we know .... To indiscriminate eulogy we are always averse; but this is a production which cannot be too strongly recommended."—*Monthly Review,* December, 1824.

An Abridgment of ZUMPT'S LATIN GRAMMAR for the use of Schools. By the Rev. JOHN KENRICK, M.A. 12mo. 3s.

EXERCISES on LATIN SYNTAX, adapted to ZUMPT'S Grammar. By the Rev. JOHN KENRICK, M.A. 8vo. 5s.

Books printed for B. Fellowes.

A KEY to EXERCISES adapted to ZUMPT'S GRAMMAR. By the Rev. JOHN KENRICK, M.A. Second Edition. 8vo. 5s.

WANDERINGS IN SOUTH AMERICA, the North-West of the United States, and the Antilles. With original INSTRUCTIONS for PRESERVING BIRDS for Cabinets of Natural History. By CHARLES WATERTON, Esq. Second Edition. 8vo. 10s.

" Every page of his (Mr. W.'s) book breathes such a spirit of kindness and benevolence, of undisturbed good humour and singleness of heart, that we know nothing to compare with it, except the little volume of that prince of piscators, the amiable Izaac Walton.... His book we may safely pronounce to be full, not of amusement only, but of curious and useful information regarding the natural history of the equinoctial regions of South America."—*Quarterly Review*, No. 66.—See also the *Edinburgh Review*, No. 86.

The LAWS of the CUSTOMS, compiled by direction of the Lords Commissioners of His Majesty's Treasury, and published by the appointment and under the sanction of the Commissioners of His Majesty's Customs; with Notes and Indexes. By J. D. HUME, Esq. Controller of His Majesty's Customs in the Port of London. 8vo. 1l. 3s.

www.ingramcontent.com/pod-product-compliance
Lightning Source LLC
Chambersburg PA
CBHW080051190426
43201CB00035B/2165